The Hospitality Masters Series

Read what the industry is saying about these books:

They fit the way we operate in the 90's. They are fast-paced and packed with hard-hitting tidbits. In just a few minutes, I can pick up a great idea and get back to work!

Greg Hunsucker, Co-owner
V's Italiano Ristorante, Kansas City, MO

What a great idea! I can't tell you how many management books I have started and never finished. These have exactly the sort of information I can really use - concise and to the point.

Mark Sneed, Director of Operations
Phillips Seafood Restaurants, Washington, DC

You can't miss with advice from the best of the best! I like that these books don't preach. They credit me with enough intelligence to be able to adapt these ideas to fit my particular situations. Why didn't somebody do this sooner?

Mark Valente, Owner
Marc's Restaurant, Wheatridge, CO

These books contain practical ideas in an easy-to-read format that can help any operator increase sales, reduce costs and improve profit margins. They are useful books for any food professional from multi-unit director to small kitchen manager.

William Dillon, VP for Market Development
ARAMARK Campus Services, Philadelphia, PA

The Hospitality Masters Series

An invaluable collection of insights and experience from professionals who understand our business . . . filled with some simple "how to" solutions.

Marjorie Mintz, VP Human Resources
The Levy Restaurants, Chicago, IL

A super-concentrated collection of immensely valuable sales and profit-building ideas. These books are truly a tremendous resource to anyone in the hospitality industry.

David Newton, Director of Operations
Applebee's, Pittsburgh, PA

These are the perfect resource for busy food & beverage executives. Every page is loaded with common sense that I can put in my managers' hands for quick training of important issues. It's like a total Restaurant University in a book!

Greg Gallavan, F&B Director
Winter Park Resort, Winter Park, CO

As the owner of a restaurant, I am always searching for ways to improve my sales and profit. [These books] are practical and effective tools for my management staff and myself to use for continual growth and success.

Chris Shake, Owner
The Fish Hopper, Monterey, CA

These books are filled with clear, concise advice that can definitely increase the bottom line. I have read industry books twice the length with half the insights.

Richard Ysmael, Corporate Director
Motorola Hospitality Group, Schaumburg, IL

CONTRIBUTING AUTHORS:

Gloria Boileau
Internationally-recognized professional speaker specializing in
environmental enhancement, image and communications

Susan Clarke
Internationally recognized as the #1" high energy/high content speaker
author on attitude, employee motivation, customer service and sales

Barry Cohen
Award-winning chef, national speaker and
CEO of Old San Francisco Steak House

Howard Cutson, FMP
Principal of Cutson Associates and a sought-after speaker
on customer satisfaction and beverage operations

Tom Feltenstein
The nation's leading authority on
foodservice and hospitality marketing

Peter Good, FMP
Nationally-recognized motivational speaker and
trainer to the hospitality industry.

Jim Laube, CPA
President of the Center for Foodservice Education
and consultant in profitability and financial management.

Bill Main, FMP, FCSI, CSP
Nationally-known author, consultant and speaker and
Past President of the California Restaurant Association

Phyllis Ann Marshall, FCSI
Principal of FoodPower, specialist in concept development,
growth strategies, and merchandising with food and menus

Bill Marvin, The Restaurant Doctor™
The most-booked speaker in the hospitality industry,
author, consultant and advisor to operators around the world

Rudy Miick, FCSI
Nationally known consultant in hospitality operations
and performance improvement

Ron Yudd
Director of Food Service for the United States Senate Restaurants
and an experienced speaker, trainer and motivator

**Tested ideas from the leading speakers and
consultants in the hospitality industry**

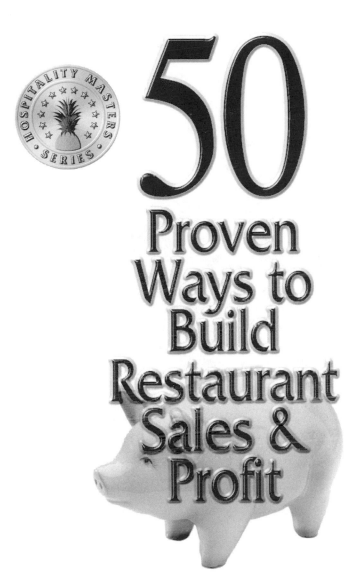

50
Proven Ways to Build Restaurant Sales & Profit

Edited by
William R. Marvin

Hospitality Masters Press
PO Box 280 • Gig Harbor, WA 98335

This publication is intended to provide accurate and authoritative information in regard to the subject matter covered. It is sold with the understanding that the publisher is not engaged in rendering legal, accounting or other professional services. If legal advice or other expert assistance is required, the services of a competent professional person should be sought.

Photo Credits
  Page 125 – Lucien Capehart Photography, Palm Beach, FL
  Page 127 – Terry Blackburn Photography, Houston, TX
  Page 130 – Stegner Portraits, Colorado Springs, CO

Library of Congress Catalog Card Number: 97-70023

ISBN 0-9656262-0-2

ATTENTION ASSOCIATIONS AND MULTI-UNIT OPERATORS:
Quantity discounts are available on bulk purchases of this book for premiums, sales promotions, educational purposes or fund raising. Custom imprinting or book excerpts can also be created to fit specific needs.

For more information, please contact our Special Sales Department Hospitality Masters Press, PO Box 280, Gig Harbor, WA 98335 (800) 767-1055, e-mail: masters@harbornet.com, Fax: (888) 767-1055.

CONTENTS

About the Hospitality Masters Series 1
Introduction 3

PART 1
BUILD SALES

1. Marketing: keep it in the neighborhood 7
   Tom Feltenstein
2. Get flexible, get cozy, get wealthy! ...., .. 9
   Phyllis Ann Marshall, FCSI
3. Expectations: the key to guest satisfaction 11
   Susan Clarke
4. Pre-shift sales briefing ,. ...., ... 13
   Bill Main
5. Build sales through environmental enhancement ... 16
   Gloria Boileau
6. Start a late night menu 19
   Bill Marvin, The Restaurant Doctor
7. Change your menu to spark customer traffic 21
   Tom Feltenstein
8. "WOW" your sales: the ZORK interview 23
   Barry Cohen
9. Wine sales for dummies 25
   Howard Cutson, FMP
10. Pick a signature item and grow for it! 27
    Phyllis Ann Marshall, FCSI
11. Making discounts work 29
    Tom Feltenstein
12. Your uniforms leave a lasting impression 31
    Gloria Boileau
13. The specialty drink menu 33
    Howard Cutson, FMP
14. Tap the power of sampling 35
    Bill Main
15. Build sales by creating more value 37
    Susan Clarke

16. Stop wasting . . . people! 39
    Phyllis Ann Marshall, FCSI
17. Be #1 without being #1 41
    Tom Feltenstein
18. Sales mix: a tool for creating profit 43
    Ron Yudd
19. Alcohol-free alternatives 45
    Howard Cutson, FMP
20. Lunch on the Fast Track 47
    Jim Laube, CPA
21. Put empty space to use 48
    Phyllis Ann Marshall, FCSI
22. Color influences buyers 50
    Gloria Boileau
23. Scripting and role play 52
    Bill Main
24. Zone merchandising 54
    Tom Feltenstein
25. Build loyalty, not the check average 56
    Bill Marvin, The Restaurant Doctor

PART 2
CONTROL COSTS

26. Beat the clock to raise productivity 61
    Jim Laube, CPA
27. Position descriptions that improve productivity 62
    Bill Marvin, The Restaurant Doctor
28. Checklist for a profitable purveyor relationship 65
    Ron Yudd
29. Garbage – a blinding flash of the obvious 67
    Bill Main
30. Improve beverage controls 69
    Howard Cutson, FMP
31. Lower Worker's Comp premiums 71
    Jim Laube, CPA
32. Purchasing for profit 73
    Ron Yudd
33. Change your work week 75
    Bill Marvin, The Restaurant Doctor
34. Avoid the great bartender rip-off 77
    Howard Cutson, FMP
35. Develop inventory stats 79
    Jim Laube, CPA

PART 3
ADOPT PROFITABLE IDEAS

36. Screen applicants, not applications! 83
    Peter Good, FMP
37. "WOW" your staff: create psychological ownership . 85
    Barry Cohen
38. Open your books to maximize performance! 87
    Rudy Miick, FCSI
39. 24-hour recruiting 89
    Peter Good, FMP
40. The power of presence 91
    Bill Marvin, The Restaurant Doctor
41. "WOW" your community 93
    Barry Cohen
42. Hire your way to profit! 95
    Rudy Miick, FCSI
43. Just say charge it! 97
    Jim Laube, CPA
44. "WOW" management: just TEAM it! 98
    Barry Cohen
45. The wrong trainer 101
    Peter Good, FMP
46. Hiring a bartender 103
    Howard Cutson, FMP
47. The menu gauntlet: only the strong survive 105
    Ron Yudd
48. Employee evaluations in 10 minutes or less 107
    Peter Good, FMP
49. Higher motivation=lower turnover +more profit . . 109
    Susan Clarke
50. Art & Science 111
    Rudy Miick, FCSI

APPENDIX

Appendix A – Author background information 117
Appendix B – Recommended reading 129
Appendix C – Offers you can't refuse! 130

ABOUT THE HOSPITALITY MASTERS SERIES

You may have heard the old exchange:

Q: What is the secret of success?
A: Success comes from good judgement.
Q: Well, where does good judgement come from?
A: Good judgement comes from experience.
Q: OK, but where does experience come from?
A: Experience comes from bad judgement!

The joke would be funnier if it weren't so accurate!

Have you noticed that the School of Hard Knocks has a high enrollment? When wrestling with a problem, have you ever wished you could pick the brain of an industry expert who has "been there and done that" instead of just volunteering for yet another "valuable learning experience"?

Well, that is precisely the purpose of the Hospitality Masters Series of books.

We tapped the leading consultants and speakers in the foodservice and lodging industries for their most successful ideas on a series of topics essential to success in hospitality.

Hospitality Masters Press was formed to collect these gems, distilled from years of industry experience with their own (and other's) triumphs and tragedies, and present them in bite-sized pieces that even the most harried manager can quickly digest and apply.

The consultants, speakers and authors whose ideas are collected here are the best of the best in our business. At any meaningful gathering of industry leaders in North America, one or more of these experts is probably sharing insights in a standing-room only seminar or workshop.

When the leading operators in the US and Canada look for professional counsel, these are the names on the "short list." Our contributing authors produce the tapes that encourage and inspire thousands and write the books that become standard industry references.

50 Proven Ideas to Build Restaurant Sales and Profit is the first in a most valuable and exciting series. We welcome any comments you may have on this book as well as your suggestions for future titles.

We believe the books in the Hospitality Masters Series will become must-have additions to the professional library of every foodservice and lodging executive.

We think you will agree.

INTRODUCTION

Profitability is the interaction between income and expense. If you can increase revenue or lower costs, you are likely to have more money on the bottom line. If you can do both, you are guaranteed more profit.

Increase sales
The most immediate way to build the bottom line is to boost sales. You do not have a cost problem that cannot be covered by higher volume. In the pages that follow, you will find tested ideas to help you gain more sales from your existing customers as well as powerful ways to bring in new patrons.

Control costs
The other piece of the profitability puzzle is costs. Nobody ever got rich by saving money but you can not afford to waste your resources. Because this book is intended for the seasoned manager, we did not spend time writing about more conventional ways to control costs (like portion control.) You should already know about things like that. The cost control section includes potent but less obvious ideas on how to save money and get more bang for your buck.

Adopt profitable ideas
Finally, because hospitality enterprises are organic entities, the book includes a few ideas that are a bit more on the philosophical plane to help start you thinking on a more productive level. If you can allow yourself to open up to some new directions, you may be surprised at the possibilities you will start to see.

About this book

This is not a "how-to" manual. In fact, you may find seemingly contradictory ideas in here. The industry experts we have gathered in this book cannot tell you how you should run your business – the goal is only to share ideas that have worked for others. You must decide which ones, if any, are appropriate for you.

Each thought in this book has been condensed to its bare essence so some may raise more questions than they answer. If this happens, the contributing authors can provide more clarification . . . but only if you ask! Contact information is included in Appendix A.

How to use this book

This book is a collection of bullet-proof ideas from battle-tested veterans – use it that way. Keep it close and refer to it often. Ideas you are not ready for today might be perfect answers a few months from now.

Get copies of this book for all key members of your management team and have pass-around copies for your staff. The cost is minimal and the potential gain is huge. (Helping others to make you more money is a very smart thing to do!)

A closing thought

Good ideas won't you make rich – it is only the **application** of good ideas that will make life better. This book should make you think. Ultimately, the real power in these ideas may not be in the ideas themselves, but rather in the insights each might trigger for you. We hope you will adapt these notions to fit your needs and take them to a new level! Good luck!

Part 1

BUILD SALES

1
MARKETING: KEEP IT IN THE NEIGHBORHOOD

Imagine a circle around your restaurant with a radius of three miles. Now, imagine that everyone outside that ring disappears. You would hardly notice the effect on your business!

Our research shows that nearly 80% of restaurant sales – whether a one-store independent or a member of a major chain – come from within the three mile radius that represents your neighborhood. Are you directing 80% of your marketing efforts toward that critical area? Or even 50%?

The mass marketing myth that the more people you reach, the more business you will attract just does not work for neighborhood businesses like restaurants. The battle for the heart, mind (and pocketbook) of the local patron must be won block-by-block, store-by-store and purchase-by-purchase through what we call neighborhood marketing.

The neighborhood marketing process begins with four key functions which will provide the data you need to target your activities:

Define your customers
For each meal period, find out who your customers are and where they live and work. Over a two-week period, ask all guests for their home and business zip codes. Record the information by meal periods and transfer the

totals and percentages to a local zip code map. You may be surprised at the results.

Identify potential promotion partners

Promotion partners are retailers, groups, fund-raisers or facilities you can team with to share customers through cross-promotion. For example, you might distribute a ticket discount that drives diners to the local theater. A discount for after-the-show ticket stubs can drive theater-goers to you.

Identify community events

Certain community events are potent sales and/or business-building opportunities – parades, concerts, fairs, walk-a-thons, etc. Check your local Chamber of Commerce for a list of activities.

Collect consumer media information

Gather data about local media which will reach potential customers in and around your trading area. Ask for rate cards as well as information on scheduling and required ad materials. Utilize your zip code research to help identify your best targets.

Completing these four functions will arm you with important knowledge to help develop and target successful neighborhood marketing programs. It is your future. Do it now!

Tom Feltenstein, an accomplished author and sought-after speaker, is hailed as the top strategic and neighborhood marketing consultant for the foodservice and hospitality industry. For more details and contact information, see Page 121.

2

GET FLEXIBLE, GET COZY, GET WEALTHY!

Guests are no longer willing to sit in dining rooms that are less than half full and too deadly quiet. (Ever notice how everyone ends up in the kitchen at parties?) Please your guests with guaranteed cozy dining and your sales will grow as a result.

Take charge

You cannot control the number of guests who arrive but you can control how full the room looks and how cozy the guests feel. It takes the willingness to re-organize your seating, the wisdom to change service policies and the ability to reconfigure the dining areas to match your volume of business. It will not happen with huge open dining rooms, rigid seating policies or by using the dreaded "This Section Closed" signs.

Take action

Here are a few suggestions:

- Organize the best seats in the house into clusters and seat them first.

- Use permanent or movable room dividers you can reposition to change the effective size of the room.

- Use visual elements like mirrors, plants, trees, umbrellas, wall hangings, curtains and art objects to break up the room.

- Change lighting levels between occupied and unoccupied seating areas.

Comfort by design

One of my most frequent recommendations in new construction (and we have often been able to do it in renovations) is to design several smaller side rooms that can be used for private dining, closed off when not needed or opened to the main dining area at peak times. If you are really ambitious, movable wall systems and alternative entrances allow amazing flexibility in utilizing the restaurants square footage while accommodating the guests' needs.

Positive changes

If you effectively use simple techniques like these, guests will seldom even notice that the room layout has been altered. In fact, the subtle changes in the look and feel of the dining area can actually create variety and warmth in the meal experience.

The safest way to build volume is to have your existing guests return more frequently . . . and guests only come back because they *want* to! The more comfortable and cozy the guests' dining experience, the sooner they will want to repeat it.

Phyllis Ann Marshall, founder of FoodPower, is a visionary who can see added profit centers in every nook and cranny of a restaurant. For more details and contact information, see Page 125.

3

EXPECTATIONS: THE KEY GUEST SATISFACTION

Hospitality is a business based on expectations. The more a consumer spends, the greater expectations he or she will have. Meet those expectations and you will succeed; exceed them and you will prosper.

Reality check

Let's say you eat out and your meal costs $5.00. What are your expectations? You expect the meal will be a "no frills" experience – ready quickly, the food hot or cold enough, probably wrapped in paper and handed over a counter to be eaten with disposable utensils in an environment dominated by plastic.

If these expectations are met, a sort of unspoken contract has been fulfilled between the customer and the restaurant. The value received corresponds with the price charged. The expectations have been met. The guest is satisfied.

Now consider a $20.00 meal. Your expectations will be both different and greater. This time you will probably expect a china plate, a tablecloth, glassware, metal flatware and personal table service.

How about a $50.00 meal? You will surely have greater expectations but now they have to do with nuance and grace. You expect the decor to be more elegant, the service more attentive, the food more fashionable. Perhaps you will expect to be served on fine china at a table covered in real linen, perhaps with crystal goblets and sterling silver cutlery. These upgrades are important because the customer expects them to be there.

No matter what the price of the meal, when their expectations are met, guests are satisfied. When their hopes are exceeded, diners are delighted!

Tune in to expectations

To assure happy guests, it is important that you understand your clientele's expectations. Talk to your guests and take cues from individual diners' reactions, requests and comments. Only when you are clear on the expectations can you hope to satisfy the unspoken contract between you.

To stay competitive in the '90's, you must stay tuned to the changing needs of your customers, cater to those needs regularly and let your staff know how vitally important they are in the process of providing value and meeting or exceeding guest expectations.

When you do this consistently, you create patrons who are loyal supporters, have no reason to go to your competition and who feel good about spending their money with you,

Susan Clarke is internationally recognized as a high energy/high content speaker on attitude, employee motivation, customer service and sales. For more details and contact information, see Page 118.

4
PRE-SHIFT SALES BRIEFING

In most, if not all full service operations, one area of opportunity to build volume lies in increasing sales through improved selling skills at the table.

There are virtually hundreds of tactical ideas to assist the waiter or waitress in selling more. But to really make a difference, today's operator must focus on selling strategies that unfold within the restaurant's four walls, from the time that a guest crosses the threshold until leaving the building.

A realistic goal is to improve communication between the management, the kitchen team and the server salespeople who are actually talking to the patrons.

Knowledge is power
The better equipped servers are to explain, promote and merchandise food items - whether the core menu or specials - the more they will sell. Tips will be incrementally higher, add-on sales will build and extra profit will be banked.

The approach is to create an environment conducive to selling, replete with information and data about what is being served. This can be best accomplished by developing an effective pre-shift sales briefing. Most operators have a short meeting with the waitstaff before each meal to relay the specials and describe the fresh or in-season menu items. No big deal.

But it *is* a big deal. Because to compete effectively, you must make a material investment, not in a short meeting to share information, but rather in a strategic selling session.

Structure of the meeting

I recommend a 30-minute session just before the floor opens with a well-organized agenda. Each key area is thoroughly discussed, with points of emphasis arranged logically. Having a clear format for the shift supervisor or floor manager to follow will help assure that all the servers will listen attentively.

It is imperative that the pre-shift briefing become a major priority. It permits the communication that is so crucial to success and it can increase the average check, introduce new menu items and inject interest, adventure and excitement into the dining experience.

Get your staff involved

Orient the briefing to food, beverage and service. Have the chef, lead line cook or kitchen manager introduce the specials, focusing on the unique selling propositions that make each item SPECIAL – unique ingredients, preparation methods and characteristics.

The bar manager or wine steward should introduce the wines that complement the dish properly. If you have featured before or after-dinner drinks, this is the time to introduce them. Be sure the staff knows what they are and how to describe them to the guests.

Practice the words

Finally, the meeting should cover how each item should be described to the guest and presented at the table. Servers need to know what questions the guests are likely to have . . . and the proper answers.

For example, the soon-to-be-world-famous Nebraska Smokehouse features "line caught Columbia River Sturgeon fillet, lightly smoked with alderwood, then pan seared medium rare, served with Tule Lake horseradish, mashed potatoes and steamed fresh broccoli al dente." With a description like that, do you think you could sell a few of those?

Keep the focus

The point is to use the meeting to educate your staff so that they can educate your guests. If you are willing to make the extra effort, you will be rewarded with higher price points and greater value perception. Most important, guests will perceive that your food is different, exciting, interesting and even adventurous.

The pre-shift sales briefing is the place to celebrate the magic of food, drink and hospitality; to establish the knowledge, enthusiasm and motivation necessary to sell, sell, sell!

This article is condensed from a series of Special Reports published by Bill Main & Associates. For more details and contact information, see Page 124..

5
BUILD SALES THROUGH ENVIRONMENTAL ENHANCEMENT

Did you ever think that the position of your entrance, cash register or range could impact on your sales? Surprising as it may sound, the layout of your operation may position you for profound success or endless struggle.

How does it work?
What we call environmental enhancement derives from the ancient Chinese art of object placement. Over 3000 years ago, the Chinese discovered how your working environment acts as a mirror of yourself and your life's circumstances. Challenges such as financial debt, poor morale and difficult staff relations can often be traced directly to the surrounding energy imbalances.

By tracing the flow of energy through the space, an environmental enhancement expert can locate the areas of your environment which correspond to such important issues as finances, relationships, health and career. When the flow of energy in these physical areas of the environment are obstructed or missing, the environmental enhancement consultant may recommend changes in the position of objects in the room, the correct application of color and much more to eliminate the problem.

Three case studies

Environmental enhancement may sound a bit theoretical, so let me share a few success stories to illustrate the impact of this technique:

> A San Diego area restaurant doubled its business (to $4 million) within a year after making the following environmental enhancement changes: they repositioned the entry door to be in direct view of the pedestrian traffic pattern, placed a large aquarium near the entrance to enhance prosperity, hung a moving object in the window to catch the eye of the passerby and changed their bar from a straight line design to one that was gently curving. The rounded curve created harmony and goodwill with their patrons.

> At the Singapore Hyatt, the entrance doors to the foyer and cashier's desk were originally built parallel to the main road. This position had the effect of causing the wealth to flow right out of the hotel. Once the main doors were realigned at an angle to the road and fountains built on both sides of the main doors to bring in greater prosperity, the hotel's business improved greatly.

> A well-known hotel in a major city was in trouble. The owners redecorated, implemented a new marketing plan and hired top-flight management. Nothing worked and the property was put up for sale within three years. The new owners applied the principles of Environmental Enhancement by relocating a pair of escalators which directly faced the door to a position at right angles to the entry, putting a long dormant fountain back into use and applying other techniques to retain the flow of energy within the property. This hotel now has one of the highest occupancy rates in its market.

Homework assignment

Here are a few environmental enhancement tips that you can implement today:

1. Make your entrance spacious and well-lit. Hang chimes at the entrance – their sound is more effective than large signs for attracting patrons. Staircases or escalators should not align directly with the entrance as this allows flow of energy to escape the building, resulting in a decrease of revenue.

2. Place your cash register in full view of the door. Hang a large mirror directly behind the register to symbolically double its contents.

3. The chef should be able to see everybody who is entering the kitchen. If the chef is continually facing away from the door, he or she will feel an uneasiness that can set off a chain reaction affecting the chef, the waiter and eventually the guest. If the range is in a cramped area where this situation cannot be avoided, hang a large mirror behind the range to alert the chef to incoming visitors.

Each facility has its own set of specific challenges and consulting an expert will help you assure maximum results. By following the principles of environmental enhancement, you can position your business for greater financial prosperity and better relationships with your clientele.

Gloria Boileau helps clients maximize the appeal of their businesses while increasing their financial prosperity. For more details and contact information, see Page 117.

6
START A LATE NIGHT MENU

What kind of business are you doing late in the evening? If you are like most operators, the answer is probably, "Not much." How about developing a late night meal segment to turn those wasted hours into increased volume?

A successful example of developing the late night trade comes from my current-favorite-restaurant-on-the-planet, Sunset Grill in Nashville, Tennessee. The owner, Randy Rayburn, has implemented a late night menu that has come to exceed lunch as a source of revenue. Best of all, he has accomplished this without expending a penny in advertising!

His late night menu consists of some lower food cost entrees off his regular menu and any items he wants to run out. These entrees are offered at half price from 10:00pm until 1:30am during the week and from midnight until 1:30am on Saturday night. Desserts, coffees and beverages remain at full price.

His late night sales mix is equally divided between food and beverages. Because of its structure, the late night menu only runs about four points higher in overall food cost than his regular menu.

A large percentage of Randy's late night market has become restaurant people looking for a bite to eat in different surroundings when they get off work! His staff makes it a point to inform guests about the late night deal and they, in turn, pass the word along to others. The late night menu takes a smaller kitchen staff to produce and all managers are cross-trained on pantry operations so they can cover in case a kitchen worker calls in sick.

Interestingly, Randy discontinued his early bird program when the late night menu took off. It seemed that the market could think of Sunset Grill either as a place to go early or late . . . but not both.

In Randy's case, he preferred the later business. His early evening business was building up well without any additional incentives and he found that his early diners were not particularly price-driven.

This article was adapted with permission from the book *Guest-Based Marketing* by Bill Marvin, The Restaurant Doctor. For more details and contact information, see Page 126.

7

CHANGE YOUR MENU TO SPARK CUSTOMER TRAFFIC

New menu products offer the greatest potential for restaurant traffic increases. But changing the menu must be handled properly if operators are to realize that full potential for expanding sales and profit.

For example, the dining public in Florida is older, better-educated, more nutrition-conscious and more drawn to convenience than in the past. These shifts create promising areas for light or nutritious foods, regional taste experiences, foods not easily prepared at home and take-out/delivered foods. Each can offer an advantage to the operator willing to exploit it.

We have evolved a seven-step process that will enable foodservice operators to multiply the success of new menu items almost exponentially.

The following summary will give you a general idea of the approach:

1. Product identification
What items will fit? What meal periods will it affect? What kind of diner will the new product attract and at what price? Will it work with the existing equipment and menu structure?

2. Product development
What is the product appearance, packaging and price? How well will it fit into the current system? Can you make enough to satisfy projected demand?

3. Consumer testing

Go outside your staff for objective focus group testing before offering the new product. Listen to the public. Go back to the kitchen if your results are negative.

4. Test marketing

Select test marketing times and locations that will address the development considerations mentioned under the product development step.

5. Consumer research

Once the product is in the market, continue to probe for guest reactions beyond the buy/no buy decision. Why is (or why isn't) the product selling?

6. Analysis

How far will you go to introduce and sell your new product? What are the incremental earnings and the costs (equipment, training, advertising, media, point-of-sale materials, etc.) attached to the new product?

7. Communication

Share your ideas with your entire operation, enlisting everyone's help in introducing, selling and testing reactions to the new product.

These steps may seem involved but our experience has shown that following these guidelines will keep you on the new product path to business expansion.

Tom Feltenstein, an accomplished author and sought-afater speaker, is hailed as the top strategic and neighborhood marketing consultant for the foodservice and hospitality industry. For more details and contact information, see Page 121.

8

"WOW" YOUR SALES: THE ZORK INTERVIEW

Have you ever heard of a ZORK? Probably not. A ZORK costs $250,000 and looks a lot like a ball-point pen. It is your job to sell it to a group of executives from the largest companies in the world.

Does that sound like a tough sell? Perhaps, but if you apply for a job on the service staff at Old San Francisco, be prepared to convince my managers that the ZORK is an invaluable asset, worth every penny.

The reason? If you can generate enough enthusiasm to sell a ZORK for $250,000, we are confident you will easily make the sale on a $20 bottle of wine or a five-dollar order of Bananas Foster.

The items on your menu are like the imaginary ZORK. Guests only know what you tell them, so your ability to build sales depends on your servers' abilities to sell what, to customers, are intangibles.

This is where the ZORK starts to work for us. Our check average is $28, more than double the industry norm. Does that mean our employees are more than twice as friendly or intelligent as our competition? As much as I would like to think so, they are not . . . but they do a terrific job of selling.

The reason for our success is salesmanship.

Starting with the ZORK interview, we require our staff to go a step beyond being friendly. We demand that they "WOW" guests with their description of that bottle of wine or the Bananas Foster flambé. So from the very first time they wear our uniform, they are not only focused on making our guests comfortable, but on increasing sales – theirs and ours.

The best servers are those who can "WOW" you with descriptions of things you have never tried, perhaps even things you never knew existed. (You should see the looks on some guests faces when they learn we serve emu and ostrich meats!)

The ZORK Interview reveals who the most convincing salespeople are likely to be. It also helps reinforce a simple truth: if you love people and are not afraid of an audience, you will be great, whether you are selling Cherries Jubilee . . . or a ZORK!

Barry Cohen is an award-winning chef, national speaker and CEO of Old San Francisco Steak House. For more details and contact information, see page 119.

9

WINE SALES FOR DUMMIES

It doesn't take a rocket scientist to sell more wine in your restaurant! Good thing, since most of us don't have too many of those on the service staff, anyway! But there are not any trade secrets, either. To sell more wine, you just need to do four basic things:

1. Make sure everyone is comfortable with (and skillful at) opening a bottle. Buy a $10 bottle corker and a gross of inexpensive, new corks. Recork your old bottles and require every server to open at least 100 bottles before you turn them loose on your guests.

2. Assure that your waitstaff knows how to pronounce every wine on the list. Run through the wine list at pre-shift meetings, with each server pronouncing the next wine on the list. How about a "Trivial Pursuit" challenge for servers where they match food items with the wines on your list? They should also be able to match wines with appetizers and desserts. "Which wines would you suggest with Rack of Lamb?" "What entrees go best with Robert Mondavi Fume Blanc?"

3. Be sure your service staff has tasted the wines you offer. Since wine is most often consumed with food, have them taste wine with menu items. For example, try a Pinot Noir and a Chardonnay with the salmon special and note how different the food tastes with each wine. Educate your staff so that they can educate your guests. The easiest way to encourage suggestions is just to have servers recommend their two favorite whites or their two favorite reds – but first they must find out what their favorites *are!*

4. Finally, let your guests know that you sell wine! Put the wine list on the dinner menu – or at least your 20 most popular wines. Suggest a wine under each food item (entrees, appetizers, desserts). Pre-set tables with wine

glasses and perhaps a full bottle of wine. Have a wine display in the lobby or dining room. If your local laws permit, offer a free taste when a guest is unsure about a particular wine. Better yet, sell them 2-3 "tasting portions" so they can try out some new wines without risk. Make it easy for your guests to enjoy wine . . . and they will!

If you will make these four simple efforts on a daily, consistent basis, I predict your wine sales will grow by 20-25%. What have you got to lose?

Howard Cutson is an Ohio-based hospitality training consultant, a sought-after speaker and seminar leader. For more details and contact information, see Page 120.

10
PICK A SIGNATURE ITEM AND GROW FOR IT!

This is the story of how a simple Chinese Chicken Salad accompanied by freshly baked zucchini bread built a restaurant, a banquet business and became the famous Dianne Salad of Pasadena.

The tale starts in 1978 at the Greenstreet Restaurant in Pasadena, California when Dianne, a friend of the owners, developed a knockout dressing for Chinese Chicken Salad. When they introduced the salad, everyone at the restaurant fell in love with it and shared their excitement with other guests.

The popularity of this item grew with the ladies at lunch and the businessmen watching their waistlines. The owners christened their new star the Dianne Salad and added freshly baked zucchini bread to the dining experience.

The press got wind of the salad from Greenstreet's fans and the subsequent stories increased the salad's following and reputation. As a result of the exposure generated by the Dianne Salad, Greenstreet was voted the best lunch restaurant in a popularity poll.

In 1992, the restaurant added a pick-up window so that Dianne Salad addicts could quickly satisfy their habits. As the convenience grew so did the large orders and soon the Dianne became a party favorite.

The offering grew from plated luncheons to party bags to cartons to feed 200 on 30 minutes notice!

In 1996, we revised the menu, adding all new salads and the Dianne Salad (in two sizes) is proudly and prominently displayed in a boxed center section. We also created a new combination – New York Steak and Dianne Salad – which placed the salad in a starring role on the dinner menu.

By popular demand, Greenstreet recently added a full banquet facility to provide a new place for the Dianne Salad and its friends to party!

How much salad do they sell? Weekly production exceeds 800 lb. of poached and pulled chicken, 125 lb. of warm toasted almonds, 50 cases of lettuce to be finely shredded, a truck full of mai fun noodles and cases of fresh oranges for garnish. This is all in addition to endless batches of secret dressing that is "just light enough, sweet enough and tangy enough."

So what does all this mean? We calculated that the Dianne Salad, directly or indirectly, is responsible for 30% of the restaurant's total sales! The next goal is to take the Dianne Salad, the secret dressing and the zucchini bread into retail production.

This shows what can be done with a signature salad. What is your restaurant famous for? What are you going do with it?

Phyllis Ann Marshall and her company FoodPower help restaurants mine the gold hidden in their menus. For more details and contact information, see Page 125.

11
MAKING DISCOUNTS WORK

As competition in the quick-service segment heats up, some chains are relying more and more on coupons and special discounts to draw sales. In the short term, discounting can be effective in getting consumers to try a new product but you cannot count on this tactic to achieve long term sales gains.

Discounting does not build product loyalty – its sole purpose is to drive customers into the restaurant. The rest – add-on sales, building loyalty and repeat visits – are challenges the restaurant must meet after the customer arrives at the counter.

The problem is that, over time, discounting will raise questions about your pricing structure.

For example, If an ice cream cone sells for $1.25 and you continue to offer 25¢-off coupons, you train guests that ice cream cones are worth $1.00. If such promotions go on, $1.00 is the only price they will feel comfortable paying. The trick is to discount in such a way that does not sabotage the integrity of your menu.

Rule One
The first rule of effective discounting is that, once you establish the retail price for a menu item, particularly a signature item, never discount it. A product's price is part of its position in the marketplace. Discounting it will have a detrimental effect on the perception not only of that item but of your whole store or chain.

Rule Two

The second rule of effective discounting is to never offer a promotion that weakens the credibility of your retail price structure. Create a package separate from your regular offering, one that will not negatively affect guests' perception of the value and price of the menu. In the case of new items, establish a retail price, then offer a reduced price as an introductory offer only. After a predetermined period, bring the price up to the full retail level. Better yet, offer to give away one new item free for a limited time – it will encourage people to come to your store and, ideally, lead to sales of other items.

Offering discounts to an existing customer base will not give you the benefits of increased trial or repeat business. Instead, it may erode years of positioning efforts. If you rely on discounting promotions, you must take a longer look at your operation.

Don't use discounting casually to build sales. The long-term effect will be reduced respect for your menu and pricing structure. Use discounting to build traffic during specific periods, to generate interest in new products or even newly-refurbished stores.

Remember, too, that once you get your customers in the store, it will take more than a cents-off coupon to keep them coming back.

Tom Feltenstein, an accomplished author and sought-afater speaker, is hailed as the top strategic and neighborhood marketing consultant for the foodservice and hospitality industry. For more details and contact information, see Page 121.

12
YOUR UNIFORMS LEAVE
A LASTING IMPRESSION

Nonverbal communication is six times more powerful than the words we express. This means that the image you project reflects a message that ultimately can influence the success of your business. Guests will decide on your competence and credibility within seven seconds, based upon the visual image you and your employees present.

Dress for success
Take a look at your uniforms. Does it project a specific style? Does the style complement the look and mood of the operation? Is the color flattering to the skin tone of the employee wearing it? Does it fit properly? Does it allow the person to express their uniqueness?

The style of your uniforms expresses the image of the restaurant or hotel. For example, the staff at a Mexican-themed operation might wear ethnic garb consistent with the restaurant's decor. Congruency in style will elicit a positive response from your guests and you will be perceived as consistent in your work.

Living colors
Each of us has a spectrum of color which is ideally suited to our own natural coloring and it is important to stay within your own individual color spectrum When you do, you look healthy, rich and energetic.

You deliver a subliminal message of harmony and strength. When you are not within the appropriate color spectrum, you convey a look of sallowness, disorder and ill health – definitely not the image you want to project to your paying customers.

Choose wisely, choose well

Here are some guidelines in the choice of uniforms:

1. Jackets, pants and skirts should be solid color with prints only in the tie or blouse. Navy and teal are the most widely accepted colors and most appropriate to all classes of people.

2. The uniform should fit – not only in size but in look as well. A long jacket elongates and slenderizes the silhouette while short jackets make most people look wider. Wearing dark colors on the bottom makes the individual look taller and thinner.

3. Appropriate accessories give the outfit a completed look and provide an effective way for your staff to express their uniqueness. Give your employees some guidelines and allow them to make the choice. When employees are allowed to make choices about the uniform they are more invested in the process and will take more responsibility for projecting a positive image.

When your visual image is positive and consistent, guests feel more comfortable, have a more pleasant experience and are more inclined to linger. You work hard to create a pleasant ambiance. It is only smart to select uniforms that will maximize your image . . . and your sales!

Gloria Boileau is an internationally-recognized professional speaker specializing in environmental enhancement, image and communications. For more details and contact information, see Page 117.

13
THE SPECIALTY DRINK MENU

Do you want to boost your beverage alcohol sales by 30-50%? If you will take the time and expend the effort to create a truly exciting drink library, you can sell more beverages, control inventories, raise check averages and build more satisfied guests at the same time. (And you can even get some assistance from your suppliers if you ask 'em!)

Here are some key factors to keep in mind when designing specialty drink menus:

Stay focused
Remember your overall concept and the clientele you want to attract. What are your guests currently drinking and how can you upgrade those drinks? Could you make that Margarita a "Gold Standard Vodkarita?" Could your Bloody Mary become a "Hot-as-You-Can-Make-It Mary?" You want drinks that fit your concept and are memorable to your guests.

Build in the Ooh! factor
Use interesting, distinctive glassware and colorful, fresh, oversized garnishes. You want drinks to draw attention when they are carried through the room. Listen for guests saying, "Ooh! I want one" or asking, "Ooh! What's that?" Look for a spontaneous positive reaction when the drink is placed in front of the guest. If you are not hearing those "Ooh!" comments, re-work your drink presentations until you do!

Be realistic

When you develop your list, keep in mind the skills of your bartenders and the limitations of your bar equipment. Drinks that take too long to get from the bar or which are inconsistently prepared just will not be suggested – or sold – to the guest!

Integrate the drink list

The best way to sell more drinks is to build the drink list into your food menus. Give each drink a colorful name and a tantalizing description. Do not forget the classic cocktails – they are making a big comeback!

Include pre-dinner suggestions on the appetizer menu. Devote a portion of your dinner menu to the wine list. Build an after-dinner drink library into your dessert menu. This way your guests will be thinking of their beverage choices when they are making their food selections. Now if your service team remembers to simply recommend their favorites . . .

By the way, have you ever sat at the bar of a Planet Hollywood and watched the service bartender? Every other order is one of their signature drinks . . . at prices ranging from $5.50 to $13.95! Wouldn't you like a piece of *that* action?

Howard Cutson is a customer satisfaction consultant specializing in bar operations and creative service training. For more details and contact information , see Page 120.

14
TAP THE POWER OF SAMPLING

Sampling is the purest form of menu merchandising possible. Enticing the guest with a complimentary sample of a menu item appeals to all of the senses – taste, sight and smell. Tantalizing those taste buds creates an impulse buy situation that keeps guests coming back for more.

There are five important points to manage to assure successful sampling:

1. Designate a server
Choose one person from each shift to interact with the guests and offer the samples. You want an outgoing person - usually a server, skilled busser or food runner - who loves people, has a ready smile, a generous nature and loves to have fun. In addition to a higher hourly wage, you may also offer them a bonus for every order purchased as a result of their product introduction via sampling.

2. Use special serving pieces
Purchase special platters with colorful artwork that corresponds to the theme of the food being sampled. Heavy southwestern platters with cactus and chili pepper artwork can be used when sampling Mexican cuisine. A heavy white platter with a decorative blue design will nicely accentuate a sampling of Jumbo Sea Scallops in a special marinade.

3. Pay attention to presentation

Serve sampled items in small portions that are easy to handle. Try to create small plates to share. There is no better way to introduce the fun of sampling than by creating a mini-event in which all guests in a party participate. People love to give their opinions and the objective views of your guests about new food items is powerful information.

4. Create a unique uniform or dress designation

A special hat, sash, apron, button, wristlet, choker, tie or shirt for the server will make the sampling process fun, interesting and visually exciting. A young woman in a sailor's hat presenting samples of deep fried clams or a male bartender in a tuxedo offering a new line of domestic caviar, will help energize your guests around the food.

5. Develop and practice the verbal script

This is show business. With your "sampling team," discuss how guests should be approached, what should be said and how responses should be framed. Then take the time to actually practice the narrative at least ten times before going out on the floor. Have the sampling interns discuss which script sounds the best – it must come across naturally to give credibility to the product being sampled.

Everybody loves something for nothing and offering guests samples of your featured items can prime the pump for increased sales.

This article is condensed from a series of Special Reports published by Bill Main & Associates. For more details and contact information, see Page 124.

15
BUILD SALES BY CREATING MORE VALUE

Operators keep saying that times are tough in the '90's. Between the "perceived" recession and the "reality" of all your competition, I can understand why they might feel that way . . . but they are wrong!

Stop whining!
Times are only tough for operators who are not focused on the primary reason they are in business – their customers! Customers pay your rent and put food on your table. Whether you sell cots, cocktails or calamari, you are in the people business - and if you don't like people, you will soon have no business.

No slack
The customers of the '90's are less inclined to give your business a second chance than they were a decade ago. Today's diners have less money to spend and less time in which to spend it. This means that the block of time they allot for dinner at your restaurant is perceived as more precious than ever.

Create value
Our industry is based on a very simple proposition: people want to get "perceived" value for the "reality" of the money they spend. They can count the reality of what they pay out, but value exists in a kind of perceptual gestalt – the whole is always far more than the sum of its parts.

Value has three components, the blend of which creates the customers perception of quality: product, service and atmosphere.

Quality product
Think of your product in a broad, encompassing sense. Product is everything you sell: food, beverages, rooms or whatever. Having a quality product requires that you be constantly improving and working on it. Are you?

Quality service
Service is about how you and your staff accommodate the guests. It must be prompt, courteous, competent and just a little bit better than your competition. Don't worry about being miles ahead – just a few steps ahead can make you the restaurant of choice.

Quality atmosphere
Atmosphere is a combination of your tangible physical assets and the intangible ways they affect your customer. The personal atmosphere that you and your staff create is more important than the design and fixtures. It is a "positive energy flow" that occurs when every member of the staff and management exudes positive attitude and acts like he or she truly cares about every guest.

When you are focused on the needs of the guest and you are consistently providing quality and value in your product, service and atmosphere, your guests will get that satisfying and comfortable feeling that makes them feel truly welcome and eager to spend money with you.

Susan Clarke is internationally recognized as a high energy/high content speaker on attitude, employee motivation, customer service and sales. For more details and contact information, see Page 118.

16
STOP WASTING . . . PEOPLE!

There is a new meaning for waste management: maximizing your human resources – utilizing the talents of your staff (and your labor dollars) to increase productivity, quality, pride and profits. To illustrate, let me share a case study from Mr. Stox Restaurant in Anaheim, California:

The situation
The holidays were approaching and the owners wanted to corner more market share by offering outstanding variety in the bread basket (the first item to the table) and to knock guests' socks off with memorable desserts (the finishing touch).

The challenge
To do this, they would need a talented, creative pastry department – a pastry chef plus two assistants – but they would also have to increase payroll substantially to produce items that would not yield much revenue. The bread basket did not generate any extra dollars; the dessert prices were fairly fixed and often included in banquet pricing. At this point many restaurants would throw out the idea as impractical!

We brainstormed the situation and found . . .

The solution
We added another profit center - retail - at the greeter stand where the popular breads could be sold to go.

The pastry chef developed chocolate caramel almond brittle with a 30-day shelf life. The management team branded the candy by placing it in special containers with elegant Mr. Stox logo stickers. They sold these handsome tins at the greeter stand during Christmas.

The results

Creating an attractive display in the front of the restaurant and selling handmade breads and candy paid for the development of the recipes and the staff to produce the products. Distribution requests came in from local gourmet stores and now Mr. Stox has 20 commercial accounts – a major branded marketing arm of the restaurant – that generates goodwill, name recognition. . . and about \$30,000+ a year!

The bottom line

You can pay for (and keep) better people if you have more work for them to do. An effective way to build this additional business is to utilize your excess labor hours to create memorable products, items you can use in the restaurant and market in many other ways to enhance your image and increase total sales.

When faced with the possibility of excess labor hours, don't waste people or cut payroll, expand sales!

Phyllis Ann Marshall is a chef herself with creative knowledge of the possibilities with people, equipment and facilities. For more details and contact information, see Page 125.

17
BE #1 WITHOUT BEING #1

You can be number one! That does not necessarily mean being the biggest or most profitable restaurant in town. Rather, it means identifying an opportunity and doing a better job with it than anyone else.

In marketing circles, this approach is called "niche marketing." The trick is to find a niche in which you can simply be better than anybody else and exploit that position to achieve maximize growth.

If you have already done this, you know that achieving this kind of domination and growth requires mental concentration. The greatest mistake in most growth strategies is to try to expand into too many areas.

There are four primary ways in which you can claim a niche and differentiate yourself from the competition. The greater your separation from the pack, the more your chances of success. This requires a meaningful difference, not a rehash of "me-too" ideas.

1. Determine the market
Choose a group of consumers that you can turn into devoted fans by appealing to them in a unique way. You must answer the question, "Who can I serve as Number One and how will I do it?" For example, you could become known as the healthiest place in town, the best place for families, the most romantic spot or the best dining value in the neighborhood.

2. Create the experience
Produce a "special kind of experience" consumers get

when they visit your restaurant(s). This comes from what you can provide that is different and distinctive in service or product or a combination of them both. Don't hide your differentiation. Go public to gain and maintain your niche. You would be surprised at how many firms defer or under-do the advertising and promotion it takes to own their niche.

3. Control your niche
Control has to do with the penetration of new units, filling in the gaps on a calculated basis. Cultivate strong relationships with your operators/managers to keep informed of new opportunities. New market penetration requires constant monitoring – do not leave it to chance.

4. Establish value
Do not get into heavy discounting to undersell the competition. No one can have the lowest price all the time but you can always give added value for the price you charge. Price and added value can be sold just like your differentiated product or service. You must build and enlarge the perception that what you offer the customer is worth more than you are charging.

The opportunity to dominate the market in a territory that you select is up to you. With courage, foresight, and the determination to create and sell your own niche, you really can be Number One!

Tom Feltenstein, an accomplished author and sought-afater speaker, is hailed as the top strategic and neighborhood marketing consultant for the foodservice and hospitality industry. For more details and contact information, see Page 121.

18
SALES MIX: A TOOL FOR CREATING PROFIT

Monitoring your sales mix on a regular basis will give you a valuable tool that can assist you in eliminating menu losers while enhancing the winners. The sales mix helps you analyze what your guests like and dislike about your menu, tells you what items are selling and at what price and provides valuable data for future menu decisions.

A sales mix is simply a record of sales per menu item that shows how the items in each category relate to one another. To illustrate, here is a sample sales mix for a four-item appetizer menu:

ITEM	SELL	NO. SOLD	SALES
Nachos	$6.95	10	$ 59.50
Buffalo wings	$5.95	15	104.25
Mini pizza	$5.50	15	82.50
Spinach dip	$4.95	20	99.00
TOTALS		60	$345.25

Most computerized point-of-sale systems can be programmed to generate this information in as much detail as you want. Sales mix data provides the menu maker with the following information:

Popularity
Sales mix figures will show you the popularity of an item as it relates to other selections in its category. In the example above, the spinach dip sells twice as many orders as the nachos.

Price points

Sales mix data helps you identify how much the guests like to spend in each category. Our sample sales mix shows that sales of specific appetizer items decrease as their price increases. However, guests do not seem to make a distinction between $5.50 and $5.95. This helps you identify more profitable ways to structure your menu for enhanced guest appeal.

Preferences

The sales mix shows the types of foods that guests are choosing – poultry vs. beef or pastas over seafood. Trends can be easily discovered and used to create new menu items.

Planning

The sales mix also provides a way to estimate the sales of individual menu items based on projected daily sales. For example, let's say that past record-keeping indicates that 20% of your total food sales are represented by appetizer sales. Your food sales projection for the coming week is $30,000. You can safely project appetizer sales of about $6,000.

Your sales mix shows that Buffalo Wings comprise 30% of the dollar value of appetizer sales, so you can estimate $1800 in wing sales. At a price of $5.95, you now can project sales of 300 orders of Buffalo Wings next week, a great help when planning your purchases and scheduling prep staff.

Ron Yudd is an experienced speaker, trainer and consultant who helps operators design profit strategies and re-energize their passion for service. For more details and contact information, see Page 128.

19
ALCOHOL-FREE ALTERNATIVES

At a time when overall alcohol sales are virtually flat, smart operators are creating increases in beverage sales by capitalizing on the hot no-alcohol category. We have seen clients take alcohol-free sales to over 10% of total sales with very little effort! Here are a few thoughts to help you maximize no-alcohol revenue:

Virgin specials
How about alcohol-free versions of your best-selling signature drinks? Whether kids, non-drinkers or designated drivers, everybody likes something special – the alcohol content is not required. Bonus: selling a special drink instead of soft drinks or coffee keeps you from having to offer those expensive free refills!

N/A beers and wines
These are a must-have category! Carry at least one American product and one import – more is better. Your staff will get questions, so be sure they have tried the products and can describe them clearly.

Coffee
Coffee is hot (no pun intended!) Get serious about it! Use high-quality beans and grind them immediately before brewing. Use colorful, over-sized cups. Offer a selection of special and flavored blends. Don't just serve coffee, develop a coffee *program*. In most markets, an espresso machine is still one of the best investments you can make – provided your staff is

well-trained in product knowledge and correct brewing procedures.

The key to coffee sales growth is guest education. To reduce the fear of trying something new, offer a card entitling guests to try specialty coffee drinks for the same price as a regular cup of coffee. Once they understand the difference, they will be hooked!

Teas
Don't forget about tea! Offer a selection – flavored, decaf, herbal, hot, iced, spiked, bottled, freshly-brewed, make-your-own, etc. You will improve guest satisfaction and add to incremental sales.

Juices
How about fresh-squeezed juices – orange, lemon, lime, grapefruit? What about pineapple, mango and even papaya? They create a quality image, give your drinks a distinctive flavor profile and even add color to your back bar. The premium that you can charge for them adds up as well!

Water
Most servers still pour ice water before attempting to sell an alternative. Offer a selection of bottled waters at reasonable prices and you will be surprised what you can move – still waters, sparkling waters, spring waters, glacial waters, flavored waters, imported waters and hundreds more! Mention the options before automatically reaching for the water pitcher!

Howard Cutson is Principal of Cutson Associates, a customer-service focused consulting firm based in Hudson, Ohio. For more details and contact information, see Page 120.

20
LUNCH ON THE FAST TRACK

Time is everyone's most precious asset, particularly at lunch. Guarantee that your lunch customers will get their food served quickly and you may serve more lunch customers as a result. Here is how it works:

Using a sign or banner, announce something like "FAST TRACK LUNCH – served in 15 minutes or it's FREE!" Buy plastic stop watches (about $5 at Wal-Mart) to place at each table. After customers place an order, the server starts their stop watch. The food must be delivered to the table within 15 minutes or lunch is on the house.

You may want to limit the offer to certain menu items, modify the allowed time when appetizers are ordered with an entree or exclude parties over a certain size. The fewer restrictions, the more potent the offer.

The risk, of course, is that you could lose your shirt if you do not have your act together. However, if you cannot deliver food promptly at lunch, it is already costing you money – you just don't know how much!

The upside? Some operators I work with report lunch sales increases of 30-40% – more than enough sales to offset the risk of giving away a few meals!

This idea is taken from the seminar "How to Improve Restaurant & Foodservice Profitability" presented by Jim Laube, CPA, founder of the Center for Foodservice Education. For more details and contact information, see Page 123.

21
PUT EMPTY SPACE TO USE

To turn vacant chairs into cash, develop a plan to attract private parties, banquets and off-hour business meetings. The sound of a guaranteed number of guests at a fixed price is sweet music to the ears of all restaurateurs. It also provides the restaurant with exposure to new guests and sets the stage for off-site catering.

Where to start
A great place for many restaurants to start building banquet and private party business is with Saturday weddings. If your banquet space can be configured to open onto a garden-like patio room for both the ceremony and reception, you have got a gold mine! Weddings can be scheduled regularly Saturdays from 10am until 4pm. The profit on this business is sizable and the favorable exposure to a large number of potential customers (particularly the young adults) will help keep your restaurant growing.

Tools to build business
Your toolbox should include: hotel style stanchions to announce the name of the function (they can also display a generic message promoting your banquet facilities), handsome chairs and tables, good table coverings, easily convertible flower arrangements, flexible lighting on dimmers, buffet service trays and chafing dishes. You can often save money by buying these used from a rental company's stock.

External marketing

Several of my clients have established a part time marketing position to help book functions to fill their empty seats. We usually structure the job as minimal wage against a percentage of sales. This is a perfect post for someone who wants to do most of their work from home. Look for a past staff member who has left to raise a family or perhaps a retiree in the area.

Internal marketing

Include information on your banquet services as a table tent, include a mention on the menus, put a poster in the lobby. Make a professional presentation in the hallway leading to the restrooms. Any area of the restaurant where guests linger is prime space to let them know what you have to offer.

Phyllis Ann Marshall helps independent restaurants and small chains who wish to grow. For more details and contact information, see Page 125.

22
COLOR INFLUENCES BUYERS

McDonald's sells billions of burgers. Their success is due, in part, to the colors they use to influence their patrons to buy.

The psychological effect of color is profound – it is the first item the brain perceives. Your decor, menus, product design, packaging, displays, brochures and advertising all make a statement about your business to customers. Your choice of color can enhance or detract from the persuasiveness of your business, so it is important to learn to use color effectively.

Scientists are continuing to study the power of color and the way it works but there is ample evidence that color affects blood pressure, mood, eye movement, body temperature, respiration and glandular activity – effects that are subconscious and uncontrollable.

Here are some guidelines to remember when working with color.

Navy is the most acceptable color to all classes of people and is universally accepted throughout the world. Use it when you want to appeal to a general mix of customers.

Black, conveys strong authority and power. It can often intimidate people unless softened by another color.

The color **white** is emotionally negative by itself because it is perceived as bleak and sterile. Balancing it with another color makes it more pleasing.

Red is the most dominant and dynamic of all colors. It vibrates 12% faster than any other color and increases the nervous tension which creates action. Red can be very effective when you want a response from your customers.

The color **yellow** is considered energizing and cheerful. It stimulates learning, especially when used in its clearest, brightest tone.

Green, especially a grass green, is a balancing color. The color green reduces nervous and muscular tension.

Here are some tips for accurate color usage:

1. White walls with a red or black accent are the best color combination in the kitchen. The white will show off the colors of the food.

2. The restaurant dining area may be multicolored but do not exceed more than three colors or the brain will have a hard time. Dining room colors should create a feeling of pleasure, comfort and happiness. Avoid using red in the bar area because it can inspire an argument.

3. Outside signage should be brightly colored and moving, if possible, to catch the eye of the customer. Red and yellow is always a winning combination – it creates the illusion of time slowing down. Yellow makes the person feel cheerful and red gets them into action. Suddenly the customer is in your restaurant, not at your competitors'. Just look at McDonald's colors!

The conscious selection of color is critical to the success of your business. Used correctly, color will give you the competitive edge and will increase your sales in today's fast changing environment.

Gloria Boileau is an internationally-recognized professional speaker specializing in environmental enhancement, image and communications. For more details and contact information, see Page 117.

23
SCRIPTING AND ROLE PLAY

Effective training builds sales. Scripts and role play are a great way to train service staff, greeters and bussers. Here are three good examples from the soon-to-be-world-famous Nebraska Smokehouse:

Greeters
A new host is in training. It is his third night on duty, but his first alone at the front desk in the main entry. He practiced the correct telephone answering script repeatedly in training. In this case, the appropriate telephone response is: "Good evening, Nebraska Smokehouse, home of hickory smoked Prime Rib! May I help you?"

Now the supervisor can observe the host actually answering the telephone to be sure the trainee is familiar with how the words flow and that his delivery sounds natural. Three repetitions is usually enough to determine if more training is needed.

Bussers
Bussers are responsible for pouring water at table side. It is late spring in Nebraska, so ice water is being requested more and more frequently. At the pre-shift briefing, the manager demonstrates and discusses the proper pouring techniques:

* refill the glass only when the water level is 50% or lower
* leave ½" at the top of the glass to avoid spillage
* whenever possible, pour from the left of the guest

These three points of water service can detract from the total dining experience if not executed correctly. During the pre-shift meeting, each busser can easily demonstrate his or her water-pouring technique in 1-2 minutes. Practice does indeed make perfect.

Servers

The servers at the Nebraska Smokehouse want to build a devoted following of guests who ask for them personally. Moreover, the restaurant's marketing plan specifies a significant investment in a frequency program, which builds loyalty buying patterns and focuses on return business.

The pre-shift briefing is used for role-playing a very effective guest communication discipline – don't just thank the guests when the check is paid and the meal has ended, invite them to return.

The script could look like this: "Thank you very much. Please come back and see us, and ask for me personally." Servers should repeat this phrase, or variations on this idea, aloud several times until they are comfortable and the delivery feels natural.

Your goal is to create consistently, not robots, so give your crew some latitude. If you do not give your staff direction, they will just make something up! Used properly, scripts and role-play help your staff better understand what you want and how to deliver it.

This article is condensed from a series of Special Reports published by Bill Main & Associates. For more details and contact information, see Page 124.

24
ZONE MERCHANDISING

To succeed in the foodservice marketing game, focus your efforts on consumers within a 10-minute drive time of your restaurant. These people make up 75% of your customer base. An incredible 87% of quick-service diners travel only three to five minutes to eat.

What this means is that, if you are smart and do not have unlimited funds(!), you should spend your marketing dollars within your four walls, inside your property line and in your immediate neighborhood.

The place to begin a productive marketing campaign is right inside your restaurant – a concept known as "four walls marketing" – with a powerful technique I call zone merchandising.

Divide your restaurant into merchandising zones – essentially message centers from which you can send signals to your customers. Zone merchandising will turn your restaurant into a medium within itself – one that is far more effective than radio, television or print.

Here are just a few examples of sales opportunities within your restaurant's merchandising zones:

Lobby zone: decals, easel posters, suggestion boxes, danglers

Front counter zone: register toppers, brochures, matches

Bar zone: posters of dramatic drinks, point of purchase (point of persuasion) opportunities

Dining room zone: special boards, danglers, table top displays, menus, napkins, wine lists, after-dinner treats

Bathroom zone: point of persuasion opportunities, newspapers, music

Employee zone: pre-shift meetings to encourage team work, uniforms, selling suggestions

Kitchen zone: incentive contests

Valet zone: greeters, vacuuming card, thank you cards, windshield washing

Drive-thru zone: streamers, windshield washing, menus, handing out doggy bones

Delivery and carry-out zone: car signage, take-out menus

Office zone: messages on hold, answering machine, telephone scripts

Parking lot zone: landscaping, cleanliness

Property line zone: banners, awnings, sandwich boards, marquees

When planning merchandising zones, remember that what the eye sees, it buys. To catch the eye of your guests, make your displays colorful and creative.

Effectively implementing neighborhood marketing methods such as zone merchandising has enabled many restaurants to increase sales as much as 10% within 120 days.

Tom Feltenstein, an accomplished author and sought-afater speaker, is hailed as the top strategic and neighborhood marketing consultant for the foodservice and hospitality industry. For more details and contact information, see Page 121.

25
BUILD LOYALTY,
NOT THE CHECK AVERAGE

Let's say your typical guest comes in twice a month and your average check per person is ten dollars. Let's also say that you would like a 50% sales increase (who wouldn't?) What are your options?

Option 1: Increase the Check Average
You could try to increase your average check to $15 and hope that people would still come in as often as they did before. You might be able to pull this off but I would not want to bet on it.

Most operators tell me their guests have a certain amount they are comfortable spending in any given situation. Pressure to increase the per person expenditure could result in lowered guest counts. Raising the average check is not likely to work.

Option 2: Invest in Promotion
You could invest heavily in promotion but promotion can also be expensive. Every cost you add raises the sales required to net out a 50% increase. Besides, the odds of coming up with a campaign that would produce a consistent 50% sales increase are also pretty slim. Promotion is usually not the answer.

Option 3: Increase Frequency
What are the odds that you could treat your guests in such a way that instead of coming in twice a month,

they would come in three times a month? Pretty good, I'll bet.

Just one more visit a month would provide that 50% sales increase . . . without any increase in average check and without any increased pressure on the guests or your service staff! If you can give your guests such a good experience that they come to you instead of patronizing your competition, you cannot help but increase your volume.

The secret is frequency
You see how it works? A 50% sales increase seems impossible, but getting guests to come back one more time a month seems pretty reasonable. And it is. After all, your guests are eating *somewhere*, why shouldn't it be with you?

Even if guests come in twice a *week*, one more visit a month is still a 12½% sales increase, again without any pressure to increase the average check.

Focus on delight
So the safest way to achieve sales growth is to have your guests return more often. In this mode, your goal is to delight your guests, win their trust and earn their loyalty rather than simply trying to increase the average per person sale.

Don't get me wrong – if a guest wants to spend more money, I have no problem in taking it with gratitude and a smile! But it is about time we stopped having such a fixation on how much our guests spend on each visit and started putting our energies toward increasing the number of times they visit!

Higher checks are OK, but . . .

Now the two are not necessarily incompatible – it is possible to build both repeat patronage *and* the check average. However, I place the focus on the human side of the equation because foodservice is a business based on personal relationships.

I do not believe that success in building the average per person sale will guarantee guest loyalty or repeat patronage nor will it necessarily sustain long term sales growth.

On the other hand, I firmly believe that success in building guest loyalty and repeat patronage will always increase total revenue and sustain it over the long term.

This article was adapted with permission from the book *Guest-Based Marketing* by Bill Marvin, The Restaurant Doctor.   For more details and contact Information, see Page 126.

Part 2

CONTROL
COSTS

26
BEAT THE CLOCK TO RAISE PRODUCTIVITY

Many operators report a steady decline in the general work ethic among workers. To light a fire under newly hired workers, here is a technique that can help build time awareness and get new hires in particular more productive in less time.

Have new staff members wear a plastic stop watch around their necks for the first few weeks of training. Whenever the trainee begins a task (like prepping 20 pounds of shrimp or bussing and resetting a 6-top), start the watch. When the task is completed, stop the watch. Compare the elapsed time to a standard for performing the task. Each person can keep track of their own times so they can see their progress.

In any event, staff members "on the clock" know the watch is ticking and someone is going to notice. It can also be motivating for workers to beat their own – and their co-workers' – best times.

Of course, you must monitor performance to be sure that short-cuts are not taken at the expense of quality. However, if applied properly, this approach can help your staff develop an appropriate sense of urgency and achieve higher productivity in less time.

This idea is taken from the seminar "How to Improve Restaurant & Foodservice Profitability" by Jim Laube, CPA, founder of the Center for Foodservice Education. For more details and contact information, see Page 123.

27
POSITION DESCRIPTIONS
THAT IMPROVE PRODUCTIVITY

Position descriptions are like a road map to your organization – properly constructed, they help your staff find their way and better understand the game you are asking them to play.

The problem with most job descriptions is that they are little more than lists of activities ("do this, do this, do this"). I call these activity-based job descriptions since they focus on the activities that we want people to engage in.

I have worked in operations with activity-based job descriptions and had to conduct evaluations for workers who were performing poorly. They invariably defended their behavior by showing how they had, in fact, done every task on their job descriptions. This is akin to claiming to be the world's greatest lover by virtue of having memorized the manual. It is also about as effective!

Marvin's Law of Creative Laziness says that you never do any more work than is necessary to accomplish the results you want. In this spirit, I suggest that you (and your staff) will be better-served if you define positions in terms of *results* instead of *activities.*

Defining results allows people to interpret their jobs in a way that works for them. The immediate advantage is increased productivity, enhanced guest service, improved morale, reduced turnover . . . and more constructive performance appraisals!

A results-based position description has the following four sections:

Position Summary
This is a succinct statement of the reason the position exists at all! For example, my server description (I call them service managers) is summarized as "Delights restaurant patrons with responsive food and beverage service."

Essential Professional Functions
These are activities required in the successful performance of the position. A server's professional functions include selling and serving food and beverages to guests in the dining room and bar, making change, clearing and resetting tables and so forth.

Results Upon Which Performance is Evaluated
This is the real meat of the approach – results by which successful performance will be measured. For a server, these might include "guests regularly ask for this person's station, guests are acknowledged within one minute of being seated, stories of this person's legendary service abound and similar results.

Qualification Standards
These are the basic physical requirements of the position in compliance with ADA guidelines.

What makes results-oriented position descriptions unique is the ability to define and measure results as the primary means of performance appraisal. They also make performance review more of a coaching exercise and less of a personal confrontation.

Admittedly they take some time to refine and it is important to review them carefully before you use them to be sure they do not call for standards you are not prepared to uphold.

Better yet, review them with your staff and agree what is possible! For example, when a client in Portland, Oregon opened a new restaurant, he made results-based position descriptions an integral part of his staff training.

He spent two days with his new crew to reach a consensus on their jobs. They discussed the results needed from each job and agreed on measurements that would tell if they were achieving those results. He said he was gratified to discover that his new staff had standards that equaled or exceeded his own!

Managers tell me that managing results is easier and more fun than watching activities. They have found easier ways to get the work done and improve the flow of service to the guests. Best of all, they tell me that staff productivity increases 10-20%!

This material was adapted with permission from the book, *The Foolproof Foodservice Selection System* by Bill Marvin, The Restaurant Doctor. For more details and contact information, see Page 126.

28
CHECKLIST FOR A PROFITABLE PURVEYOR RELATIONSHIP

Establishing a positive relationship with a purveyor will make your job easier and enhance your opportunities for profits. The following checklist will help you select the right vendor in the first place, review existing purveyors and assist in evaluating new relationships.

❏ **REPUTATION**
How is the purveyor viewed by other food service buyers?

❏ **SERVICE**
What is the level of service that this purveyor provides and how does he react when you need emergency service?

❏ **PRODUCT PRICE**
Are this purveyor's prices competitive in the market? Do they buy in sufficient volume to keep prices low?

❏ **QUALITY**
Does this purveyor provide the quality level you demand?

❏ **CLEANLINESS**
Are you able to visit the purveyor's plant or warehouse? What is the condition of the purveyors warehouse and delivery vehicles?

❏ **BID PRICE AND INVOICE PRICE**
Does the purveyor charge on the invoice the price that was quoted in the bid?

❏ **QUANTITY PURCHASED VS. DELIVERED**
Are there discrepancies between what was purchased and what was sent on a delivery?

❑ **FREQUENCY OF DELIVERY**
Does the purveyor's delivery and frequency meet your needs and preferences?

❑ **PERSONNEL**
Are you receiving the level of service that you desire from the sales, ordering and delivery personnel?

❑ **MARKETING/MERCHANDISING SUPPORT**
Does the purveyor have a system to help you promote the food you purchase? Are point-of-purchase and other merchandising materials available? Are recipe materials available and provided? Can they provide financial or other assistance in producing menus? Do they have marketing dollars to invest in promotion?

❑ **PRODUCT CONDITION**
Is the condition of the delivered product as requested? Is the product delivered at safe and proper temperatures? What is the condition of the shipping container? Does any product appear to have been repackaged? How frequently has product had to be returned?

❑ **CREDIT FOR RETURNED PRODUCT**
What is the response or the level of difficulty in receiving credit for products that are returned to the purveyor?

Select purveyors as carefully as you would choose a business partner, for that is what they are. Any good partnership is built on shared expectations and open, honest communication.

This material is adapted from Ron Yudd's program, *200 Points of Profit.* Ron is an experienced speaker, trainer and consultant. For more details and contact information, see Page 128.

29
GARBAGE - A BLINDING FLASH OF THE OBVIOUS

Food cost has a profound affect on profitability in full service restaurants. Solid systems are important to food cost control but the proper training of the food preparation staff is equally critical.

In my experience, as many as 10 points can lie between the theoretical (ideal) food cost and the actual food cost generated from physical inventory. For many restaurateurs, these dollars make the difference between success and failure (or between making the bank payment or not!)

A restaurant kitchen is a manufacturing plant. Raw materials are purchased, broken down, processed and fabricated for retail sale. If you believe your specifications and portions are correct, the next place to analyze is the procedures used in preparation.

Don't look over the shoulders of prep cooks to see if an 8-ounce fillet of fish really is 8 ounces and don't personally check to see that raw carrots are trimmed to ensure maximum yield. If you had that kind of time, you would do the job yourself.

Instead, modify your employee's behavior. You want to ensure that prep cooks break down raw products correctly because, whether you are there or not, they know their work will be checked.

How can this be done? ***Remove the garbage cans from your kitchen!***

In their place, substitute plastic bus tubs and place them strategically throughout the prep area. Instruct the prep crew to deposit all trimmings, cuttings and paper waste in the tubs.

Put a tub rack or baker's rack in a conspicuous place and have employees place their filled tubs in the rack. At the end of the shift, you or your kitchen supervisor personally checks the contents of the tubs to ensure proper preparation procedures are being followed and raw products are being correctly trimmed.

This changes the psychological mind set of hourly preparation workers. They can no longer throw food waste into a garbage can, never to be seen again. They become accountable for their work, because it can be monitored.

Showing a prep cook the amount of usable waste in their tub has a dramatic impact. This direct feedback positively affects behavior, work attitude and morale. It is also an excellent tool for performance evaluation.

The best result? I have found that this technique can lower food cost by 1-2% almost immediately. This proves it – there's gold in those garbage cans!

This article is adapted from Bill Main's top-rated seminar *Profit Tools.* For more information and contact information, see Page 124.

30
IMPROVE BEVERAGE CONTROLS

In our ***Beverage Controls Workshop,*** we spend over three hours honing in on the basic control cycle in our efforts to improve beverage profits. If we were to highlight the single most important point in each step of the control cycle, they would be the following:

Par stocks
Establish effective par stocks for your storeroom and each bar...and live by them.

Receiving
If you do not have a true Receiver, have one person in charge of receiving all your beverage stocks. Train that person well in the Items you carry. Don't forget, Robert Mondavi makes more than one type of wine!

Storage
The *last* person who should have a key to the liquor storeroom is the bartender . . . and a good bartender does not want one anyway! Restrict key access to no more than two managers.

Issuing
No matter how small your operation, always use requisition forms to create a paper trail. Have the manager and the bartender sign off on the delivery to the bar and always be sure to use an empty-for-full bottle exchange.

Standardized recipes

Standardized recipes are the basis for any effective control program. However, over half the people who attend our workshops do not have them. Without recipes, all of your control efforts are wasted. Every bartender *must* make your drinks according to *your recipe!* The bonus is that your drinks will taste great, no matter who makes them!

Receiving Payment

Make sure every item served from your bar is properly rung on a check. Never allow "bunching" of drinks or "make-up" rings. Use a change box with a ten-dollar bank to eliminate the need for "no sale" rings.

This material is taken from a half-day workshop entitled *Effective Bar Cost Controls* offered by Cutson Associates. For more details and contact information, see Page 120.

31
LOWER WORKER'S COMP PREMIUMS

A safe working environment is not only the right thing to do for your staff but it can also add more dollars to your bottom line. Fewer on-the-job injuries lead to lower premiums on your Worker's Compensation coverage . . . month after month after month.

Here are just two things that you can do to help reduce your Worker's Comp premiums:

Enforce a no-cut glove rule

Make a company policy that says when doing kitchen prep, anyone with a knife in one hand must have a nylon, no-cut glove on the other hand. It is virtually impossible to cut yourself when wearing a no-cut glove. No-cut gloves can be purchased from most distributors. When purchased in bulk, you can get the cost down as low as $3.00 each.

Your people can place a plastic glove over the no-cut glove when going from product to product to prevent cross-contamination.

Some operators report that no-cut gloves are even more important in the dishroom where you often have younger, less-experienced people constantly cleaning large blades and heavy slicing equipment. Wearing no-cut gloves on both hands can prevent potentially serious cuts and injuries.

Have a shoe policy

Insist that everyone wears shoes with slip-resistant soles. Falls are the most common accident in foodservice. Back injuries resulting from these slips are among the most debilitating in our industry. From an insurance standpoint they can also be very expensive.

Require that the entire staff, including managers, wear shoes with a slip-resistant sole. Before and after studies show dramatic declines in slips and falls when people wear shoes with slip-resistant soles.

These shoes come in a variety of styles and colors and look just like any other type of shoe. They are, in fact, multi-functional, meaning that your people can wear them comfortably to more places than just work.

This makes it possible to require that everyone on your staff wear shoes with slip-resistant soles and not have to pick up the cost as long as you provide them with at least two sources to purchase the shoes. Some companies advance the money for new staff members to purchase their first pair and get it back through payroll deduction.

These shoes cost no more than comparable shoes. Look for manufacturers and distributors in industry publications and check out discounters like Wal-Mart and K Mart for the best prices.

These ideas are taken from the seminar *How to Improve Financial Management & Controls* presented by Jim Laube, CPA, founder of the Center for Foodservice Education. For more details and contact information, see Page 123.

32
PURCHASING FOR PROFIT

There can be no assurance of profit at the end of the preparation and service steps of the meal without careful attention to the steps of profitable purchasing. To be assured of purchasing the highest quality at the very best price, you must take a focused approach to the way you acquire product. Here are some ideas:

Specific Specs
Put every item you purchase through a review process to determine exactly what you need to produce the final product for the guest. Write out the specific use of each product. Determine in what form it should be purchased (bulk, prepared, portioned). The more you know about exactly how the product will be used, the better buyer you will become. A detailed spec will also help improve communication with your vendors.

Quality
Determine the level of quality needed for each item you use. Buying only the highest quality sounds like the right approach (generally speaking it is) but often, because of the way it will be used, the highest quality is a waste of money. For example, you do not need Grade A lemons to make lemonade but they would be very appropriate for lemon wedges to serve with the trout. Buy broken tomatoes for the marinara sauce rather than breaking up whole tomatoes. Don't buy more quality than you really need.

Bid System

You must determine your standards regarding price, quality and service but no matter how they rank, it is important to solicit bids from various vendors. Regularly bids will help you achieve the best service, highest required quality and the most favorable price. I recommend perishables (meat, seafood, produce) be bid weekly. Grocery and non-food supplies can be shopped less frequently, perhaps monthly, quarterly or annually. Have a consistent bid system in place and gather price information frequently.

Par Stocks

Only buy what you need to last between deliveries, a task made easier by establishing par stock levels. When a par is followed, items are in the house for a minimum time so the quality does not have a chance to deteriorate. Lower quantities on hand mean less chance for pilferage. Par stocks assure that you only purchase the amount of each item that you will need for production, freeing up cash that would otherwise be tied up in inventory. Determine par levels by reviewing your recipes and projecting the sales level and product mix between deliveries.

Buying builds inventories. Purchasing, on the other hand, builds profitable restaurants.

This material is adapted from Ron Yudd's program, *200 Points of Profit.* Ron is an experienced speaker, trainer and consultant. For more details and contact information, see Page 128.

33
CHANGE YOUR WORK WEEK

You could be creating inescapable overtime just by the way you structure your work week! Like so many problems in our industry, overtime can be caused by a common practice that you probably have never thought about. Here is how the problem is created and what you can do about it:

The situation
In most restaurants, the pay week runs from Monday to Sunday. Friday and Saturday are clearly the busiest nights. It is understandably easier to deal with payroll after the weekend rush but this structure can automatically raise your payroll costs.

The problem
If you are heavy on hours by the time you get to Friday, you are in trouble. You cannot reduce labor on the weekend because you need everybody you can find to handle the crowd, so you are forced into scheduling overtime.

It is easy to rationalize weekend overtime because you are making more money and can afford a few extra bucks in payroll. Still, I believe you should never waste time solving a problem you can eliminate! Why spend the money if you can avoid it?

The solution
The answer is simply to change your work week!

If your pay week started on Wednesday or Thursday, you would get your busiest sales period out of the way when you have plenty of slack on hours.

After the busy weekend, if you found that you were a little over budget on labor, you could more easily trim hours on those slower midweek days with less risk of reducing the level of service to the guests.

This article was adapted with permission from the *Home Remedies newsletter* by Bill Marvin, The Restaurant Doctor with thanks to Mark Sneed at Phillips Seafood Restaurants. For more details and contact Information, see Page 126.

34
AVOID THE GREAT
BARTENDER RIP-OFF

"There is no such thing as an honest bartender!" I have heard this cry so often that I am tempted to believe it! In reality, I suspect most bartenders are trustworthy but good systems are the best way to keep honest people honest.

By having specific, enforced policies and by "working" your operation throughout your business day, you can prevent 90% of most potential problems. Here are a few ideas that are effective and easy to implement:

Bottle marks
Use bottle marks or stamps to ensure that all stock behind the bar is actually *yours*. One of the easiest ways for bartenders to beat you is to bring in their own products to sell to your customers.

Tip jars
Keep tip jars at least 3 feet from your cash register to prevent your bartender from confusing the two!

Lunch breaks
Pull lunch breaks for the bartender yourself from time to time. It is a great way to keep up your bartending skills and stay in touch with your guests. It also gives you a leisurely half-hour to see what is really going on behind the bar!

Mid-shift audits

Pull an occasional mid-shift audit. Read the register and pull the drawer and closed-out checks. Leave behind a partial bank. Do these regularly for all your bartenders so they will understand it is a standard practice, not an accusation.

No free drinks!

. . . at least not from the bartenders! Only the owner or manager should buy drinks for guests. After all, it does come from "the house." As a side benefit, it gives you a great reason to meet your guests. Have your bartenders point out guests they feel deserve a special treat . . . and make sure they tell you why.

Guard your guest checks

Treat your guest checks – new and used – like cash. They should have your logo on them and be serially-numbered. Always use a lock box for used checks and chits. Re-using the same chit over and over is the easiest way to rip you off. Over a 3-month period, our mystery shoppers witnessed this practice in over 85% of our shops!

Many managers ignore the bar and lounge operations because they mistakenly think they will somehow manage themselves. A little time and attention on your part will yield results directly on your bottom line.

Cutson Associates offers full and half-day bar management programs across North America. For more details and contact information, see Page 120.

35
DEVELOP INVENTORY STATS

Keeping inventory levels at a low, yet adequate level is a key element to control your food and beverage costs. Problems like over-portioning, spoilage, theft, excessive trim. waste and general carelessness toward your costly products are common when you gain too much inventory.

All operators take inventories, but most just use the figure to compute their food cost for the period. In so doing, they miss out on a valuable tool.

Get more bang for the buck
A great way to get more value whenever you price out a full inventory is to calculate the number of days' sales represented by your stock level.

Let's say you do a physical inventory of all your food products at the end of a 30-day month. The dollar value of your ending inventory is $10,000 and your overall food cost for the month is $30,000.

First, compute your average daily food cost for the month. Take your food cost and divide it by the days in the period ($30,000÷30 days=$1000). In an average day that month you used $1000 in food.

Next, figure the number of days' sales in inventory. Take your ending inventory value and divide it by your average daily food cost ($10,000÷$1000=10 days).

In this case, you had 10 days worth of food on hand at the end of the period. To most operators this would indicate excess inventory and be a signal to re-examine par levels product by product.

Rules of thumb

Following are some general guidelines on how much inventory (in number of days' sales) many operators find acceptable:

Full Service, Full Menu Restaurants
Food: 6-7 days
Liquor: 10-15 days
Beer: 7-10 days
Wine: 25-45 days*
* may vary greatly depending on size and type of wine list

Quick Service, Fast Food Restaurants
Food: 3-5 days

Some operators figure the number of days' sales on hand every week and use it as part of the incentive system for their chefs and ordering personnel. They have trimmed their inventories to the lowest possible levels which frees up cash, assures fresher ingredients for their guests and lower food costs for them.

These ideas are taken from the seminar *Ammunition to Win the Food Cost War* presented by Jim Laube, CPA, founder of the Center for Foodservice Education. For more details and contact information, see Page 123.

Part 3

ADOPT
PROFITABLE
IDEAS

36
SCREEN APPLICANTS, NOT APPLICATIONS!

With the challenges we have attracting and retaining good employees, it makes no sense to get people to fill out an application and then never talk to them! Why? Because when their applications are screened, they do not make the cut. This makes as much sense as spending a fortune to attract guests to your restaurant then giving them bad food and service.

Rationale
The reasons for screening applications sound good

"I don't have time to interview everyone who applies."
"Why interview someone who is not likely to succeed?"

but if you are not talking with people because their applications are "questionable," you are probably making a big mistake. In fact, you might be throwing away gems just because they have not been polished.

Here is a little self-evaluation exercise to help you check yourself:

Super sleuth
Do you ever take out your magnifying glass and shout "Aha! Another red flag?" There are lots of red flags in those applications – job gaps, short tenure, cut in pay, going down instead of up the ladder. So what? There might be good explanations, but you will never hear them unless you ask the person.

English teacher

Do you get out your red pen and start marking up the application? [by the way, never write on someone's application . . . it could be used against you in court.] "Just look at that poor grammar" you think, "and the spelling is horrendous!" Stop it! These applicants are probably not Ph.D. candidates . . . but how much academic prowess does it take to handle a five-table station on a Saturday night?

Check out your assumptions

If you do not believe that there are good – even great – applicants behind those weak applications, give it a test: give blank applications to your best three staff members and ask them to complete the forms. Explain what you have in mind or they will probably think you are nuts!

Take the completed applications back to your office and give them a good hard look. Are there any red flags?? Do you see any errors, omissions or other reasons not to interview these people? Probably, but these folks have proven to be successful and you would be lost without them!

Keep this experience in mind when you are in the midst of the selection process. The best workers do not always look the best on paper. Be smart. Screen applicants, not applications.

Peter Good is founder and Principal of Peter Good Seminars, Inc., a training company primarily serving the hospitality industry. For more details and contact information, see Page 122.

37

"WOW" YOUR STAFF: CREATE PSYCHOLOGICAL OWNERSHIP

At Old San Francisco, our success ultimately depends on the thousands of small decisions our employees make everyday, not just the several big decisions handled by management.

We also realize that for these employees to be truly empowered to make the right decisions, we must provide them with an incentive to do the right thing. In other words, they must own their jobs. This is what empowers them to make a difference, to "WOW" our guests (and themselves) and make their jobs exciting.

We refer to this buy-in as psychological ownership - an intangible investment in the continued success of our business. I can show the power of psychological ownership with two contrasting examples:

Recently, a diner complimented us for exceptional service. It seemed that at the end of the meal, he realized his wallet was still in the car. He left the table and asked the valet for his keys so he could retrieve his billfold. The valet dropped what he was doing and quickly brought the car to the entrance so the guest would not have to walk. Then he re-parked the car close to the front door - a lot of extra effort for no additional tip.

Understandably, our customer was "WOW"ed.

Now a much different example: When renting a car one winter night, the clerk handed me an ice scraper. I was impressed, thinking the scraper was a courtesy for the following morning. When I got to the car, however, I found that the windshield was frozen over. The attendant was not anticipating my future needs, he was just too lazy to scrape the ice off himself!

Our valet operated differently from the car-rental clerk because he had psychological ownership. He wanted to go the extra distance. He felt responsible for his job and he knew that the quality of his work made a difference to other people. It mattered to him.

How do you give your staff psychological ownership of their jobs? Start by dealing with them like they will be around tomorrow. Treat them with respect. Get to know them as people. Listen to them and learn from them. Help them understand that the job is theirs, not yours. Have faith in them and be a role model for the sort of behavior you expect.

Just as our valet "WOW"ed our guest that day, I want to always "WOW" him with my own appreciation of his contributions and my unwavering faith in his ability to do a terrific job. What he sees is what I will get.

Barry Cohen is an award-winning chef, national speaker and CEO of Old San Francisco Steak House. For more details and contact information, see Page 119.

38
OPEN YOUR BOOKS TO MAXIMIZE PERFORMANCE!

If you want to maximize performance, take a giant leap and provide your play book to the team! That's right, open your books!

With apologies to those who may be offended by sports analogies, think about an NFL team where the only person in the game that holds the plays is the owner. Not even the coach knows what is happening. Some of the great players will have a good year based on natural talent – they may even make the Pro Bowl – but the team will never get to the playoffs! So much for football. Let's talk restaurants!

The bottom line
Operators who have implemented P&L training for the staff (as well as for management) are showing a 200-250% improvement in bottom line results! At least, that is my experience based on my work with dozens of restaurateurs. Here is why it happens:

Short-sighted thinking
The traditional rationale to not open the books is something like, "If they find out how much I am making, they will demand a raise!" or "They will never understand the numbers" or "They will rip me off!" In my experience exactly the opposite is happening to those companies confident enough to take the time to train their staff in this important area.

A test

If you still need to be convinced, try this test: ask your staff what percentage of the typical restaurant dollar they think is bottom line profit. My guess is that most answers will be between 25% and 50%!

This means that if you do not give them the facts, they think you are making 50 cents on the dollar! If you do not give them the facts, they cannot be of much help in improving profitability. If you do not give them the facts, you are standing in the way of their professional development and asking them to win the game without a play book.

Benefits

First, the staff learns what it actually takes to run a successful restaurant. By sharing information on costs and income, participants can see how the business works and what it takes to make a profit.

Sales typically increase because once people learn to read the numbers, they understand that cost-cutting is only half the battle. Hourly employees start coming up with brilliant, insightful ideas of how to build sales and reduce costs . . . and all you have to do is listen! (In my experience, the toughest part is getting you to listen, but that is a topic for another time!)

Knowledge is power. The more your staff knows what it takes to win the game, the more valuable they will be as players.

This material is an excerpt from Rudy Miick's Seminar: *Change the Game to Maximize Performance!* For more details and contact information, see Page 127.

39
24-HOUR RECRUITING

In the late '70's, I never had a problem finding good people to apply for a job. Unemployment was high, competition for staff was minimal and bodies were plentiful. The boomers were out in droves looking for jobs. People would offer bribes for me to hire them!

In the 90s – and well into the first decade of the next century – the reality is different. There are fewer young people in the workforce (1975 had the lowest US birth rate in the past 50 years) and there are more employment opportunities. Now it is the employers who are paying the bribes . . . when they can even find someone to whom they might offer the money!

And in spite of the employment issues we all know and feel, we still make a very costly employment mistake – we recruit and hire people reactively rather than proactively.

We scramble to place want ads, collect applications, interview and hire people, all on the same afternoon that an employee gives us that two-hour notice! More painful yet, we have to call home to say we will have to watch our daughter's soccer game another day.

When we recruit and hire reactively, we never recruit the best. Wrong hires are not fair to our guests, who deserve the very best we can give them. They are not a nice thing to do to ourselves, either!

We must fill jobs before they become vacant. How can you afford to do that? How can you afford not to? There are always vacancies – people get sick, take leaves of absence or just fail to show up. It is less costly to have an extra person on the payroll than to reactively hire five in a row who were incompetent!

This means you start recruiting *before* people give notice! The best employers have continual ads (both external and internal) and are constantly soliciting for good employees with their customers, vendors . . . even the health inspector. The successful manager has a mind set that the next great employee is just around the corner – maybe at the dry cleaners, the gas station or perhaps sitting in a restaurant.

When you find one of these natural talents, give them your card. Say, "I am impressed with the way you handle yourself. If you know someone *like yourself* who might be looking for an opportunity, have them come and see me." By making the approach indirect, you keep the exchange comfortable. More often than not, the star will show up, perhaps with a friend. Good people tend to hang out with good people.

Superstar managers are 24-hour-a-day recruiters! And they are getting the best people. They are being selective, creative and having fun doing it because they do not have to work under pressure or duress. These managers go to the soccer games!

Peter Good is founder and Principal of Peter Good Seminars, Inc., a training company primarily serving the hospitality industry. For more details and contact information, see Page 122.

40
THE POWER OF PRESENCE

The secret to productivity and service is presence. Simply put, presence is a state of mind that is free from distraction. Your level of presence is the extent to which your mind is not occupied with thoughts unrelated to the project immediately at hand.

Lack of presence is obvious. Have you ever been talking to someone who was listening to you . . . and then suddenly they *weren't?* Didn't you know when their attention was elsewhere? Have you talked on the phone with a person who was doing something else as they spoke to you? Even though you couldn't see them, wasn't their distraction apparent?

A distracted state of mind creates irritation in other people. It is incredibly annoying to talk to someone whose mind has wandered, yet we do it ourselves all the time. We think that the way to be efficient is to do several tasks at once. Wrong!

Presence and productivity
The truth is that you can only focus your attention on one thing at a time. For example, when you are talking with a person, there is nothing you can do at that same moment about finishing the schedule or handling any other chore on your list.

The secret to productivity is to drop distractions, focus on the immediate task at hand then move on to the next project. Presence (lack of distraction) will enable you to more accurately assess situations and deal with them efficiently . . . the first time!

Presence and service

Ours is a business based on personal connection. In my service seminars, I point out that the reason guests tip 10% or 30% depends on the level of personal connection servers create with their guests. If a server is distracted ("in the weeds"), there will be no personal connection. The guest will feel less served and tip accordingly.

Does this sound too easy? I watched a server go from making 11% and struggling to averaging over 25% and cruising the next night. A pizzeria manager who attended one of my programs called a few weeks later – over half his "people problems" had just disappeared! In both cases, I asked what they were doing differently. Each replied, "I am just *being* with people when I am with people." This is the power of a clear mind when dealing with others.

Presence is a potent quality that enhances the feeling of personal service and increases management effectiveness. As you drop stray thoughts, you will naturally become more expert with people, improve productivity, reduce stress and increase enjoyment of your life both on and off the job.

This material was adapted with permission from the book *From Turnover to Teamwork* by Bill Marvin, The Restaurant Doctor and is a component in several of his programs. For more details and contact information, see Page 126.

41
"WOW" YOUR COMMUNITY

Community marketing is more than a strategy for increasing sales, it is a definition of where restaurants fit into today's changing world. At Old San Francisco, we realize that it is no longer enough just to support those who ask for our help – we need to "WOW" our neighbors by taking the initiative ourselves.

People have become more insulated and safe within their homes. To be successful, we must penetrate those cocoons through our advertising, our concept, our employees and our actions. The most potent opportunities inevitably occur when communities ask for our help, explicitly or implicitly, in times of crisis.

Over the past 25 years, our restaurants have provided food, parties and even simple awareness when our communities needed it. The crises – stranded kids, droughts, hurricanes, tornadoes – may change, but our ability to help remains the same. And it touches people where they live, creating a bond that is far more effective than any advertisement.

Let me give you one example: In the summer of 1996, a group of teenagers from the San Antonio area were promised jobs at the Summer Olympics in Atlanta. Off they went, many spending all of their savings on the one-way plane ticket or bus fare. They were understandably excited, but when they arrived in Atlanta, there were no jobs.

Since many of the teens expected the Olympics to provide housing and were counting on their wages to pay for the trip home, they were marooned.

The community was outraged but, like the teenagers themselves, felt helpless. What they needed was a company with the resources to get these kids home. So one of the owners of our company arranged for Continental Airlines to bring the stranded youngsters back. Once they arrived, we hosted a big "Welcome Home" party for them at Old San Francisco. The local American Heart Association chapter created special "Heart" awards recognizing the wonderful spirit of these kids.

It was a big win for everyone! The community saw us as a hero and our efforts generated an inestimable amount of goodwill and publicity. The total cost? Less than one large newspaper ad.

Traditional advertising no longer has much impact because people have become numbed to commercial messages. To get through to our neighbors and give them a reason to leave the comfort of their homes to dine with us, we must learn more about them, listen to their needs and be heroes whenever possible.

People still want to be touched; it just takes a little more work to create a "WOW" reaction.

Barry Cohen is an award-winning chef, national speaker and CEO of Old San Francisco Steak House. For more details and contact information, see page 119.

42
HIRE YOUR WAY TO PROFIT!

"I can't find good help!"   "My turnover is killing me!"
Sound familiar? We spend an inordinate amount of
time fussing over our labor situation. Little surprise, it
is usually our highest cost of doing business. To help
ease the pain a bit, let me share a four-step hiring
technique that can lower turnover, increase
performance and improve your profit!

1. Let the applicants choose
Attach a cover sheet to your application that defines
why you are in business and sets your expectations of
your staff. Issue a challenge to the applicant: "If this
sounds like the place for you, fill out the application.
If not, please check somewhere else." This challenge
will eliminate 10-15% of job applicants before you
ever see them!

Have a sign up sheet for applicants to schedule their
own interviews on dates and at times that you have
established. This creates your first ability to see if the
applicant shows up at a time they personally selected!
If they are late, the excuse better be pretty good!

2. Cut to the chase
Spend your time with the applicants you want to hire
rather than those you do not. Cut off an interview if
you have a sense this is not the right person for the
position. Also do some role playing immediately. Ask
a server applicant to carry four plates or describe a list

of "evening specials" you have provided in writing. Have a kitchen applicant use a French knife to dice an onion.   Have a bookkeeper run a list of numbers on a 10-key adding machine.   You will immediately get a sense of the applicant and what they can do.

3. Ask better questions

Have the applicant provide information for you, not the other way around.   Ask open-ended questions rather than questions that can be answered yes or no. Inquire about the applicant's goals. For example, "If you could do anything in world for work, and there was nothing holding you back, what would you do?" This type question gets to the person's motivation and aspiration. You will find it much more effective to hire people that are already motivated, rather than motivating someone that hasn't a clue.

4. Define expectations

Define the specific expectations you have of each applicant as they join your team! Define your training program. Define your role expectations for yourself. This means you will have to play at a different level, but so will everyone on your team.   The effective owner/operator/manager of the future is a coach and a mentor. Walk your talk and the team will too.

Of course you will still have some turnover and there will be some applicants that squeak through. But our clients have reduced annual turnover to less than 20% and in many cases to single-digit percentages.

This material is taken from the hiring & retention seminars presented by Rudy Miick, FCSI. For more details and contact information, see Page 127.

43
JUST SAY CHARGE IT!

Here is an innovative way to pay your vendors quickly and get a bonus for doing it!

Charlie Trotter's in Chicago charges purchases from some of their major vendors using a credit card that rewards them with frequent flyer miles for the dollars they charge.

The restaurant pays their card balance in full every month, so they avoid any interest charges. But best of all, they use the card to purchase enough product and supplies to earn, on average, a free trip a week!

Everybody wins with this arrangement. The vendors improve their cash flow because they are paid at the time of delivery. The restaurant gets free travel to attend food shows, charitable events or just to reward the staff!

I think many purveyors would find a plan like this very workable. Propose the idea to your major suppliers and see what sort of reaction you get. They may never have thought of it.

The point is that you are writing the checks anyway. Why not get a few "free" trips for your efforts?

This idea is shared by Jim Laube with the permission of – and thanks to – the management of Charlie Trotter's. For more details and contact information, see Page 123.

44
"WOW" MANAGEMENT:
JUST TEAM IT!

One of the most important tasks of management is motivating employees, yet restaurateurs have one of the highest turnover rates of any industry. Why?

The most common reason is that we cannot afford to keep employees by paying higher wages and bonuses. But when it costs nearly $2,000 to hire and train a new employee, we cannot afford to accept turnover as a fact of life! Clearly, the more we can motivate our people to stay with us, the more money we will save.

Our solution at Old San Francisco was to develop self-directed TEAMs, a tool that allows us to pay our people more, keep them longer and reduce the expensive turnover rate. Here are a few examples:

Recognition TEAM
Our Recognition TEAM makes sure that no good deed, however small, goes unnoticed by fellow employees. Whether handing out a "thank-you" or throwing a surprise anniversary party for a long-time employee, our recognition TEAM does not let any staff members slip through the cracks.

Business Development TEAM
The task of the Business Development TEAM is to go outside of the business to "WOW" past customers

and potential new guests. Although their budget is small, our Business Development TEAM has made us fairly famous among local businesses, which they visit often (with free wine and cheese!) It is great to "WOW" them in the restaurant but you must have people working on the outside as well, pushing the envelope from the other direction.

Contest TEAM

Our Contest TEAM has to motivate employees on a very tight budget, so the real reward of each contest is the fun and challenge of winning. That means using low-cost incentives like lottery tickets, and contests like bingo that everyone can understand.

Our Contest TEAM devises team activity as often as possible, pairing up the most and least experienced staff for a particular task. This creates an automatic training effect, where the less-skilled employee learns to come up to the level of the more successful one.

Scheduling TEAM

We noticed that managers were spending too much time creating staff schedules that often underwent dramatic changes during the week anyway.

Now our scheduling is handled by a TEAM, using a simple rule of thumb: we divide the number of dinners we expect to serve by 20 to determine staffing needs. This means that if we expect to serve 300 dinners on a Monday night, we need 15 servers on the floor.

That number also determines how many busboys we

need, how many valets and so on. Our manager creates a simple chart and forecasts daily sales – the scheduling TEAM fills in the blanks and does the rest.

We also have TEAMs maintaining the appearance of our restaurants, hiring new staff members and doing other critical tasks. Working together for a common purpose increases motivation because it makes their jobs far more interesting and fun . . . and motivated employees stay with us longer.

Our success in reducing turnover while increasing productivity proves the equation:

TEAM = Together Everyone Achieves More

Barry Cohen is an award-winning chef, national speaker and CEO of Old San Francisco Steak House. For more details and contact information, see page 119.

45
THE WRONG TRAINER

Turnover is a huge factor in high labor costs and most foodservice turnover occurs within the first six months of employment.

Some is the result of reactive hiring decisions, some may be due to mis-perceptions of the work and some can be traced to personality conflicts. My experience, however, is that turnover within the first three months of hire is likely caused by the training program.

The problem
Even in companies that value training and commit the time, money and staff to assure that training takes place, it still fails. The problem is not with the training program, it is with us. We hired the right employee but we selected the wrong trainer!

Usually, the boss selects the best performer in a given position to train new employees in that position. This seems to make perfect sense . . . except that your best performer may be your worst trainer because they really don't want to train!

Think about it
Why would employees want to train, anyway? What's in it for them? Most of the time, nothing! They rarely get recognized or rewarded. Training will slow them down in their own jobs, which may cause them to lose money, work harder or both.

The employee may feel threatened by new trainees ("Are they here to replace me?").   Maybe the employee doesn't want a trainee to succeed for fear of losing status or benefits (best server, best stations, best days off, etc.)

The solution

As that famous swamp philosopher, Pogo, once said, "We have met the enemy and he is us!" To find the right trainer, don't ask the boss, ask the staff!

A key trait of the right trainer is that they want to train. Your staff can tell you who they go to for advice, who gives them help when they need it and who has been most valuable in teaching them new skills. In other words, they know which people on your staff are natural trainers. They may not be your most stellar performers – often they are not – but they love to train and they are good at it!

Find out who that trainer is in your business – the one who loves to help others succeed, the one with the patience of a saint, the great listener, the one with the smile, the courage and the confidence. Offer them the opportunity to earn extra money by taking on that responsibility on a more formal basis.

If they jump at the chance, they will probably succeed beyond your wildest expectations and in so doing, help you control turnover and runaway labor costs.

Peter Good is founder and Principal of Peter Good Seminars, Inc., a training company primarily serving the hospitality industry. For more details and contact information, see Page 122.

46
HIRING A BARTENDER

HELP WANTED

Psychiatric Counselor, Prestidigitator, Stand-up Comic, Efficiency Expert, Ring Master, Life-of-the-Party, Mr./Ms. Clean and Super Salesperson...rolled into one!

That's right! You need a new bartender – and you cannot afford to hire anyone but the best! If you have been over this road before, you know that those who excel in a personality position like bartender are a different type of person from your typical service staff member. Here are some hints to assure your success:

Role-play

Make the interview as interactive and job-specific as you can. Put candidates in real-life guest situations and check out their responses. Here are some sample situations:

Your guest claims you short-changed him by $10.00. How do you handle it?

A couple of guests sit down at the bar and tell you they want two beers. What do you say?

It is three in the afternoon when a neatly-dressed (and obviously intoxicated) woman in her 70s sits down and orders a double martini. What do you say to her?

To avoid any possible charges of discrimination, be sure you ask the same questions of all applicants for the position. It also helps to establish some objective evaluation criteria to compare their responses.

Put 'em to work

Schedule your interview at a time when your bar is slow. Put the candidate right behind the bar and call a typical 4-5 drink order. You will find out more in the next three minutes than you would learn in a whole hour of interviewing!

Shop them

Most bartenders are working somewhere while they look for a better job. Try to observe a candidate in his or her natural environment. Have a manager, owner or even one of your regular guests check out how the applicant conducts themselves when they don't know they are being watched. Do they keep the bar clean? Are their habits reassuring? Do they relate well with the guests? What you see is likely what you will get.

Know what you are looking for

There are specific qualities you should be looking for in that superstar bartender. Be sure your selection process addresses each of these points:

- · High energy level
- · Good speed
- · Neatness and accuracy
- · Crisp personal appearance
- · Good posture
- · Good personal hygiene
- · Comfort behind the bar
- · Smile – a big, natural one!

The atmosphere in your bar is particularly dependent on the personality of the bartender. Choose well.

Cutson Associates, offers a wide variety of bar management, management development and training workshops. For more details and contact information, see Page 120.

47
THE MENU GAUNTLET:
ONLY THE STRONG SURVIVE

The sales and profitability of a restaurant hinges on a strong menu comprised of items with real power in the market. Send every existing and proposed item through the following menu gauntlet – only the strong (profitable and attainable) will survive:

1. **Needs and Wants of the Guests**
   - Concept compatibility
   - What's hot and what's not
   - Needs of potential customers
   - Time constraint for guests – speed or leisure

2. **Cost and Profitability**
   - Cost of raw product
   - Related costs:
     - showmanship
     - service and production (labor)
     - presentation costs

3. **Quality and Availability of Food Products**
   - Accessibility
   - Understandable specifications
   - Quality from holding to production
   - Storing and handling new or unique foods

4. **Production Capabilities and Limitations**
   - Equipment: cook/hold/serve
   - Serving and display equipment
   - Utensils – production and service
   - Warming and holding devices

5. **Expertise of Staff**
   - Preparation knowledge of in-house personnel
   - Communication of ingredients/preparation methods
   - Need to instruct staff on service

6. Ability to Control
- Front and back of house supervision
- Items easily portioned
- Pre-production control
- Post-production control
- Use of food as leftover – marriage of foods

7. Varietal Balance – Each Menu Category
- Balance hot and cold
- Color – contrast and complement
- Shape and size of item
- Texture
- Preparation method
- Numerical balance – category and menu

8. Nutritional Value
- Providing an option
- Adaptability for "special diners"
- Recheck preparation methods
- Types of foods identified – fresh, frozen, processed

9. Holding Capabilities
- Does product hold well prior to consumption?
- Holding prior to service – how and where?
- Holding during service – on line – how and where?

10. Ease of Service
- Ease of service – <u>extended</u> vs. <u>solid</u>
- Are service personnel required to serve?

To keep your menu in top revenue-producing shape, perform this analysis whenever you add new items to your menu. Do it for all menu items at least once a year even if you make no changes at all. Remember that today's star can be tomorrow's dog. Be sure you identify the weak items before your guests do.

This checklist was adapted with permission from Ron Yudd's forthcoming book, *Points of Profit.* For more details and contact information, see Page 128.

48
EMPLOYEE EVALUATIONS IN 10 MINUTES OR LESS

Employee performance evaluations should be like changing the oil in a car. Everyone needs their "oil" changed every 3,000 miles or every three months, whichever comes first. Unless other repairs are needed, it should only be a 10-minute task.

Communicating with your crew will help maximize retention, promote productivity and improve morale, yet we fail to do it regularly. The longer between evaluations, the harder evaluations become. If we do performance appraisals annually, it is a confrontation that is dreaded by employee and employer alike. It is not the concept, it is the execution. Evaluations are a fantastic tool, if they are used correctly.

Frequency
Conduct evaluations every 3-6 months, not annually. Think of them like the oil change . . . the longer you wait, the more expensive it becomes. Four 10-minute evaluations a year are far more effective than an one 40-minute annual appraisal.

Documentation
Keep good records so you do not have to remember what you discussed the last time. You may conduct 50 evaluations, but for the staff member, it is only one . . . and employees always remember every detail of their last performance review.

Listen

If you have ten minutes for an evaluation, spend the first four minutes allowing the employee to evaluate their own performance. They can be pretty tough on themselves and it is better to have employees beat themselves up on their work rather than you doing it! While they are speaking, listen – really listen – to what they are saying and how they feel about it.

Coach

Spend the next four minutes on your observations of their performance and any areas you would like to see improved. Be fair. Focus on performance, not personality. Remember to praise any performance improvements that occurred since the last evaluation. Everyone wants to do a good job and no one argues with a boss who really wants to help them succeed.

Set goals

Wrap up the evaluation by mutually agreeing on goals that are specific and attainable. Agree how you will measure progress. End the evaluation on a positive, supportive note. After all, an engine should be running smoother, not rougher, after an oil change.

Why bother with the evaluations? Without direction, guidance, support, challenge and feedback, people – like cars – will burn out and break down.

Peter Good is founder and Principal of Peter Good Seminars, Inc., a training company primarily serving the hospitality industry. For more details and contact information, see Page 122.

49

HIGHER MOTIVATION=LOWER TURNOVER+MORE PROFIT

Turnover costs money . . . in recruiting costs, lower productivity and reduced service quality – money you could keep if you could keep good people longer.

People stay with you and perform at their best when they are motivated. Motivation is that drive within people that incites them to action. It is an internal process. You cannot motivate someone, people motivate themselves. However, it *is* possible to modify behavior with the right kind of incentives.

Tangible incentives
Many operators think that money is the only way to get someone to perform. While it is true that money will motivate a good majority of your people, it is short term because there is never enough of it.

There are other tangible incentives like promotions, health insurance, achievement awards, contests with prizes, educational opportunities, tuition assistance, transportation, stock options, day care facilities or even percentage ownership. But all of these come off the bottom line and that is not always easy to do.

Intangible incentives
Intangible incentives are just as motivating if not more so and they only require the investment of your time. Here are three of the most powerful:

Be appreciative

Praise and recognition for a job well done is a great behavior modifier. How often do you reprimand or correct your staff as opposed to praising them? Catch your people doing things right. Let them know how much you appreciate them and how you couldn't do without them. Tell your people how you feel and reap the rewards.

Delegate responsibility

Delegation is not about giving up your power and control – it is about giving yourself less stress, which in turn will create a more positive environment. Leaders delegate responsibility and allow their staff to be part of the decision-making process. People will motivate themselves when they are valued and have a say in their jobs.

Have fun

It is OK to have fun . . . *and* make money! Your attitude and behavior set the tone and have an impact on everyone around you. When you are having fun in your work, you allow your people to have fun in theirs as well! The more people enjoy their jobs, the better they will perform and the higher level of service they will provide.

So in addition to supplying them with the knowledge and tools to do their jobs well, express your gratitude to your staff, get them involved and provide them with the opportunity and encouragement to have fun.

They will be happier and more productive on the job, stay with you longer and make you more money in the long run.

Susan Clarke is internationally recognized as a high energy/high content speaker on attitude, employee motivation, customer service and sales. For more details and contact information, see Page 118.

50
ART & SCIENCE

To create a guest service program with more impact and effectiveness, try a little Art & Science. This new training approach is achieving spectacular results for our clients and it can help you sharpen your service as well.

What is Art?
What is Science?
Art includes all the "soft skills" of service like how you introduce yourself and the tone of voice you use. Science covers all the mechanical pieces of service like serving from the left and clearing from the right.

Most service activities involve both art and science. By defining the applicable art and science in each step of service, you will be able to train effectively in areas that were previously difficult.

Let's look at how this would apply to a full-service server position:

Art: smile, use a warm tone of voice, use a different introduction than you did at the adjacent table, use direct eye contact, stand so you can see your section while you are at the table, and similar skills.

Science: Greet the guest, introduce yourself, offer a specific beverage, suggest an appetizer selection as the guest reviews the menu, point out the specials listed on the menu, depart and place the beverage order, and so forth.

Continue this process all the way through presenting the check, receiving payment, and bidding the guest adieu. Each step of service must be identified and both its art and science components defined.

Implementing the approach
There are three preliminary steps:

> **Step 1:** Define the expectations or needs of the guest within your restaurant concept. "Our guests expect hot food, cleanliness, knowledgeable, smiling staff, pleasant attitudes and so forth. Hint: talk to your guests to be sure you are in touch with what is really important to them.

> **Step 2:** For each position, define the specific behavior required by your staff to satisfy the guests needs and expectations in terms of both the art and the science involved. Involve as many people in the organization as practicable and look for consensus.

> **Step 3:** Monitor guest comments to determine how well their expectations have been met. If you are hearing feedback like, "The place is always so clean!", "The servers are so knowledgeable." or "The staff here is always so pleasant!", you are on the right track! If not, make the necessary course corrections.

The bad news
It takes time to define the myriad of steps in the Art & Science approach. Reaching agreement on just what needs to be done, what it should look like and how you can measure it will test your leadership skills and force you to open up to new ideas and approaches from your managers and staff. It is necessarily a slower process than "my way or the highway."

The good news
The process will really make you appreciate the skills

your team has or needs to have. The process also sends a clear signal to your staff that you care about their knowledge and the guest experience. The results we have seen are improved staff retention, more specific detail about exactly what is expected from the staff and more clarity as to what is "right".

The proof of the pudding

Satisfied operators say it best. Mel Owens, CEO of Buck Owens Productions, said "We get nothing but raves about our guest service! I attribute this to our hiring process and the Art & Science approach."

My suggestion is to try it! Your guests are worth the effort and the results are worth the time investment!

This material is condensed from *The Art & Science of Quality Service©*, a system and client presentation designed by Rudy Miick. For more information and contact information, see Page 127.

APPENDIX

Gloria F. Boileau

Gloria Boileau is an internationally-recognized professional speaker and expert in environmental enhancement, image and communications. She utilizes the art of placement which enhances the flow of energy in a business. Gloria offers insightful advice on furniture placement, color, room positioning and much more. The outcome of these changes results in noticeably improved guest satisfaction and increased cash flow.

Gloria's image and communications programs are based on the powerful effects of subliminal and nonverbal communications. Implementing her proven techniques has a profoundly positive impact on her clients' sales and profitability.

Gloria is an active member of the National Speakers Association and holds a degree in communications from the University of Wisconsin. She has over 20 years experience in communication and image-related fields such as law, television, design and management. She has had numerous articles published in national magazines and trade journals.

Gloria presents enlightening, educational and entertaining seminars internationally on the following topics:
· Creating Wealth, Health and High Quality Relationships with Environmental Enhancement
· Your Visual Impact: It Can Make or Break Your Career
· Conflict Management Skills that Work
· Powerful Presentations Plus . . .

For more information, contact Gloria Boileau at:

BOILEAU & ASSOCIATES
PO Box 502 · Cardiff-by-the-Sea, CA 92007
Voice: (800) 754-0150 - FAX: (619) 730-0151
boileau@earthlink.net

. . . or circle the following numbers on the reply card:
Consulting information: (01)   **Speaking information: (02)**

Susan Clarke

Susan Clarke's success in communicating positive customer service traits is based on her life experiences. She started working in a customer service position at the age of 12 when she was hired as a "busboy" in a small family-owned restaurant. From then on, she has always been in "people contact" jobs. In 1976, Susan started with Gilbert/Robinson, Inc., the operators of Houlihan's and other restaurant concepts. Working as the corporate training coordinator, she opened over 40 restaurants nationwide for Houlihan's.

As a speaker, Susan Clarke explodes with information and motivation guaranteed to entertain, inform and inspire. She has helped restaurant, hotel, private club and public contact service leaders plan and develop new customer service strategies, staff training programs and national personnel policies.

With over twenty years experience as a trainer, manager, consultant, author and speaker, Susan Clarke's expertise in the field of guest service is truly unparalleled. Her no-nonsense approach to customer service helps service staff exceed guests' expectations by doing their jobs better and more efficiently.

Susan is the author of *The Secrets of Service: The Story of Making Your Customers Feel Good About Spending Their Money,* designed to help develop customer service skills and strengths. She shares the secrets of her own success in her book and in each of her customized presentations.

For more information, contact Susan Clarke at:

MOTIVATION UNLIMITED!
2110 Sunset Cliffs Blvd. · San Diego, CA 92107
Voice: (888) WE-MOTIVATE · (888) 936-6848
FAX: (619) 224-0902 · e-mail: MotivateU@aol.com

. . . or circle the following numbers on the reply card:
Consulting information: (03)   Speaking information: (04)

Barry Cohen

Barry Cohen leads the food and beverage industry in cutting edge marketing strategies and management techniques. His programs on "WOW" marketing are drawing crowds all over the country.

Barry has more than 20 years experience in the restaurant industry and has managed multi-unit restaurant chains in Florida and Texas. He joined the Old San Francisco Steak House Corp. as General Manager for the San Antonio restaurant in 1989. Four years later he took the helm as CEO. Old San Francisco has restaurants in Austin, Dallas, Houston and San Antonio.

Along with his corporate duties and speaking assignments, he is a frequent guest chef on local and national television programs and a regular guest host on local radio morning shows. Barry is an innovative epicurean who has received numerous awards for his original recipes, including prizes from the National Egg Council, Dole Pineapple Company and the National Strawberry Council. He placed in the "Great Chefs of Texas" competition sponsored by the Texas Dept. of Agriculture.

Among his other honors, Barry received the coveted Pinnacle Award from the Sales and Marketing Executives of San Antonio. He is an active volunteer in national and local civic organizations. Barry holds a degree in interdisciplinary business and psychology from Southhampton College.

For more information, contact Barry Cohen at:

OLD SAN FRANCISCO STEAK HOUSE
9809 McCullough · San Antonio, TX 78216
Voice: (210) 341-3189 · FAX: (210) 341-3585
e-mail: osfcorp@onr.com

. . . or circle the following numbers on the reply card:
Consulting information: (05)   Speaking information: (06)

Howard Cutson, FMP

Howard Cutson, FMP, is Principal of Cutson Associates, a customer satisfaction-oriented consulting firm serving the hospitality industry. He has spent over 30 years working in all aspects of this industry - from bartender to maitre 'd and from Assistant Manager to Director of Marketing - giving him hands-on knowledge of the daily challenges of his clients.

He is a former Vice President of Stouffer Restaurant Company and faculty member at the University of Akron, teaching hospitality management and beverage management courses. He consults in the commercial restaurant/hotel sector as well as with private clubs, health care and B&I foodservice. Howard is the author of **Hospitality Role-Play Trainer®,** a unique program to improve the effectiveness of daily waitstaff training.

His available workshops and presentations include:

Full-Day Workshops
- People Management 101
- Building Your Own All-Star Team
- Managing Today's Bar
- Taking Control of Turnover

Half-Day and Show-Length Programs
- Effective Bar Cost Controls
- Building Your Bar Sales
- Growing Lifetime Customers
- Building Employee Loyalty
- Doin' the Old Soft Sell
- Basics of Bar Hospitality
- Professional Telephone Skills

For more information, contact Howard Cutson at:

CUTSON ASSOCIATES
589 Atterbury Blvd. · Hudson, OH 44236
Voice/FAX: (216) 656-3335

. . . or circle the following numbers on the reply card:
Consulting information: (07)   **Speaking information: (08)**

Tom Feltenstein

Tom is the CEO of Feltenstein Partners, a foodservice and hospitality consulting firm focused on building sales through strategic and neighborhood marketing. He has over two decades of experience in the hospitality business and is generally acknowledged to be the industry's leading marketing authority.

Tom began his foodservice career as a senior level marketing executive with McDonald's and Burger King Corporation. He served as Senior Vice President for an internationally known billion-dollar advertising agency and later owned a chain of 14 restaurants.

Tom is Chairman and founder of the Neighborhood Marketing Institute™, a division of Feltenstein Partners. NMI sponsors the popular annual training conference, NMI Foodservice Marketing War College which has been hailed by Restaurants & Institutions magazine as "The best nitty-gritty conference on how to market a restaurant (of any kind)."

Tom is a sought-after speaker with an energetic and dynamic presentation style and has been a featured presenter at major hospitality industry conferences in the US, Canada and Europe. He is the author of several breakthrough publications and has an acclaimed series of audio and video training programs (see Appendix B). Tom's engaging wit wins over audiences around the world and has led to guest appearances on The Financial News Network and The David Letterman Show.

For more information, contact Tom Feltenstein at:

FELTENSTEIN PARTNERS
44 Cocoanut Row, #T-5 · Palm Beach, FL 36830
Voice: (561) 655-7822 · FAX: (561)-832-7502
e-mail: nmi@worldnet.att.net

. . . or circle the following numbers on the reply card:
Consulting information: (09)   Speaking information: (10)

Peter Good, FMP

Peter Good is founder and Principal of Peter Good Seminars, Inc., a training company primarily serving the hospitality industry.

Peter combines his background as an educator and trainer with more than 20 years of restaurant operations experience in casual and fine dining settings. As Director of Education for the Illinois Restaurant Association, he designed and conducted seminar programs addressing topics critical to foodservice success including customer service, employee supervision and motivation, food safety, recruitment and hiring.

He is author of the forthcoming book, *The MAGIC of Hospitality* and a highly-regarded speaker for both his information and his inspirational messages. Peter's humorous and enthusiastic approach has earned him a reputation as one of the industry's most dynamic, motivational speakers. A frequent speaker for the National Restaurant Association's Educational Foundation, his audiences include McDonald's Corporation, Sysco Corporation, Divi Hotels & Resorts and TGI Friday's.

Peter is the recipient of the Distinguished Service award from the National Institute for the Foodservice Industry. He has been designated a Foodservice Management Professional by the Educational Foundation of the National Restaurant Association and is a member of the Professional Speakers of Illinois.

For additional information, contact Peter Good at:

PETER GOOD SEMINARS, INC.
14 W. Burlington, Suite 200 · LaGrange, IL 60525
Voice: (800) 528-2190 · FAX: (708) 352-6767
e-mail: PeterGoodSem@earthlink.net

. . . **or circle the following numbers on the reply card**
Consulting information: (11)   **Speaking information: (12)**

Jim Laube, CPA

Jim Laube is president of the Center for Foodservice Education in Houston, Texas. In his many seminars and workshops, Jim integrates the financial and operational sides of the business to provide practical, proven methods to help foodservice organizations operate more efficiently and more profitably.

Jim began his foodservice career at the age of 15 working for a quick-service restaurant and earned his way through college as a server and bartender. After college, he spent 2 years with a national accounting firm, then 5 years with a regional restaurant chain. He has held responsible positions in both the financial and operational sides of the business.

Since 1993, Jim has presented to thousands of foodservice professionals nationwide. His clients include Walt Disney, Popeye's Chicken & Biscuits, Harrah's Hotels, Vail Resorts and the Society for Foodservice Management.

Full Day Programs
· How To Improve Restaurant & Foodservice Profitability
· What Every Foodservice Pro Should Know About Improving Financial Management & Controls

Half Day and Show Programs
· Profit or Loss: Are You Managing The Financial Side of Your Restaurant?
· Food Cost Fitness
· Building More Profitable Menus
· Staff Selection and Retention

For more information, contact Jim Laube at:

CENTER FOR FOODSERVICE EDUCATION
9801 Westheimer, Suite 302 · Houston, Texas 77042
Voice: (888) 233-3555 · Fax: (888) 233-3777
e-mail: jim@RestaurantOwner.com
website: www.RestaurantOwner.com

. . . or circle the following numbers on the reply card:
Consulting information: (13)   **Speaking information: (14)**

Bill Main, FMP, FCSI, CSP

Bill Main has a restaurant management company. He speaks throughout the United States and Canada. He consults on restaurant strategic planning, profitability and marketing. He writes regularly for national trade magazines. He is a dedicated member of the historic Chaine des Rotisseurs and is Past President of the California Restaurant Association. Whew!

A fifth generation Californian, he earned his bachelor's degree in economics at Oregon State University. He was a three-year All-Pac-8 halfback and draft choice for the Pittsburgh Steelers. After a brief stint as a pro, he moved from the gridiron to the grill, starting at the famed Henry Africa's in San Francisco. After a year as food and beverage director at the McKinley Park Hotel in Alaska, in 1974 he formed Oceanshore Restaurants, Inc., a restaurant management company offering a full range of services including financial and marketing consulting.

Bill has been designated a Certified Speaking Professional (CSP) by the National Speakers Association and gives over 80 presentations each year. Bill and his partner Barbara Geshekter, have written three best-selling books on training and management. He is also a foodservice management consultant specializing in strategic planning and profit improvement. He is a member of the Foodservice Consultants Society International and has been a visiting instructor at Cal Poly Pomona and the Univ. of San Francisco.

For more information, contact Bill Main at:

BILL MAIN & ASSOCIATES
2220 St. George Lane, Suite 1 · Chico, CA 95926
Voice: (800) 858-7876 · FAX: (916) 345-0212
e-mail: billmain@aol.com

. . . or circle the following numbers on the reply card:
Consulting information: (15)   Speaking information: (16)

Phyllis Ann Marshall

Phyllis Ann Marshall, Principal of FoodPower, has been a food industry consultant since 1978, involved with restaurant concepting and operational analysis. Her company, FoodPower, specializes in growth strategies for quick-service and multi-unit operators. FoodPower provides seminars for shopping center marketing directors, commercial property investors and restaurant operators. Topics include Management/Leadership Skills, Trends Review, Profitability, Team-Building, Profitability, Menu Marketing and Merchandising.

As co-owner and operator of Mr. Stox, one of Southern California's most popular restaurants, she helped create an innovative and highly-regarded dining facility which has received top industry awards. She is a frequent contributor to national food and restaurant trade publications and is the restaurant reviewer for Orange Coast magazine. She is an advisor to the University of California at Irvine in the development of a Restaurant Management Certificate Program.

Phyllis Ann holds a degree in Food and Nutrition from Cornell University. She trained in Paris at La Varenne Ecole de Cuisine, in London at Le Cordon Bleu, with chefs in Hong Kong, Madrid, Florence and Nice and with Julia Child in the US. Phyllis Ann is a member of Chaine des Rotisseurs and the Foodservice Consultants Society International (FCSI). She is certified by the Association of Culinary Professionals and is a founding member of the Association of Women Chefs and Restaurateurs.

For more information, contact Phyllis Ann Marshall at:

FOODPOWER
2463 Irvine Ave., Suite E-1 · Costa Mesa, CA 92627
Voice: (714) 646-3206 · FAX: (714) 646-1390
e-mail: foodpower@aol.com

. . . or circle the following numbers on the reply card:
Consulting information: (17)   Speaking information: (18)

Bill Marvin
The Restaurant Doctor™

Bill Marvin, the most-booked speaker in the hospitality business, is an advisor to service-oriented companies across North America. Bill founded **Effortless, Inc.**, a management research/education company, **Prototype Restaurants**, a hospitality consulting group and the **Hospitality Masters Press.**

Bill started his working life at the age of 14, washing dishes (by hand!) in a small restaurant on Cape Cod and went on to earn a degree in Hotel Administration from Cornell University. A veteran of the foodservice industry, Bill has managed hotels, institutions and clubs and owned full service restaurants. He has had the keys in his hand, his name on the loans and the payrolls to meet. His professional curiosity and practical experience enable him to grasp (and teach) the human factors common to the growth and success of every type of hospitality enterprise.

He is a member of the Council of Hotel and Restaurant Trainers and the National Speakers Association. He has achieved all major professional certifications in the foodservice industry. He is a prolific author, a featured guest on Hospitality Television and is a regular columnist in the trade journals of several industries. In addition to his private consulting practice, he logs over 150,000 miles a year delivering corporate keynote addresses and conducting staff and management training programs in the US and Canada (and occasionally Africa and Southeast Asia!)

For more information, contact Bill Marvin at:

EFFORTLESS, INC.
PO Box 280 · Gig Harbor, WA 98335
Voice: (800) 767-1055 · FAX: (888) 767-1055
e-mail: bill@restaurantdoctor.com
website: http://www.restaurantdoctor.com

. . . or circle the following numbers on the reply card:
Consulting information: (19)   Speaking information: (20)

Rudy M. Miick, FCSI

Rudy Miick is founder and President of Miick & Associates based in Boulder, Colorado. In business since 1978, his practice is focused predominantly in the hospitality industry and deals with new project development and organizational transformation within chains and resorts. Clients include family run and corporate owned entities. Miick & Associates is known for maximizing performance, profit and team spirit during what is usually considered traumatic change.

Rudy has balanced his entrepreneurial career with both practical experience and academic support. He has worked in the hospitality industry since the age of 15 and owned his first restaurant at age 24. He co-owns MiXX, a contemporary American Bistro, located in the wine country of Sonoma County, California. He holds a Master's degree in Administration with emphasis in both Organizational Management, and Human Resources from Antioch and has completed the Organization & Systems Design Program in organizational psychology at the Gestalt Institute of Cleveland.

Rudy is a Director of the Foodservice Consultants Society International (FCSI). He has served on the faculty at UCLA Extension in the Hospitality Management Program and is a featured speaker for the National Restaurant Association, the California Restaurant Association, the National Ski Areas Association and FCSI. Rudy's presentations are entertaining, relevant and challenging.

For more information, contact Rudy Miick at:

MIICK & ASSOCIATES
880 Sixth Street · Boulder, CO 80302
Voice: (303) 413-0400 · FAX: (303) 413-0500
e-mail: urspirit@internetmci.com

. . . or circle the following numbers on the reply card:
Consulting information: (21)   Speaking information: (22)

Ron Yudd

Ron Yudd is an experienced speaker, trainer and motivator with over twenty-five years of operational experience in the restaurant industry. He is Director of Food Service for the United States Senate, a post he has held since 1978. In his duties at the Senate Restaurants, he directs over 250 employees in serving over 12,000 meals per day in 14 different restaurants. Sixty percent of the Senate's $8 million in annual foodservice sales is generated from special events and catering,

Ron began teaching foodservice management courses in 1980 at local colleges and culinary schools. In 1986 he became an international instructor for the Educational Foundation of the National Restaurant Association. He continues to travel and teach a variety of profit and service-oriented courses.

As a keynote speaker, Ron has addressed prominent national and international groups on profitability, passion for quality service, training the service employee and service leadership. He combines a motivating style with practical take-home ideas that have immediate application on the job. Ron's most requested presentations include:

- A Passion for Service: Managing for the Guest
- Points of Profit: Cost-Effective Operations
- Personal and Professional Success for the Foodservice Operator

Ron is author of *Successful Buffet Management,* a textbook used extensively by chefs and catering managers, and is working on two exciting new books, *A Passion for Service* to be followed by *Points of Profit.*

For more information, contact Ron Yudd at:

10181 Nightingale Street
Gaithersburg, MD 20882
Voice/FAX: (301) 253-4728

. . . or circle the following numbers on the reply card:
Consulting information: (23)   Speaking information: (24)

RECOMMENDED READING

For readers who wish to improve their professional knowledge, we recommend these books by our contributing authors. For purchase information, please circle the numbers on the reader reply card or contact the authors directly.

Susan Clarke
(31) *Secrets of Service: The Story of Making Your Customers Feel Good About Spending Their Money,* 1991, Amerasian Press

Howard Cutson
(32) *Hospitality Role-Play Trainer®,* Cutson Associates

Tom Feltenstein
(33) *Foodservice Marketing for the 90's: How to Become the #1 Restaurant in Your Neighborhood,* 1992, John Wiley & Sons, Inc.

(34) *Restaurant Profits, Advertising and Promotion: The Indispensable Plan*

(35) *Uncommon Wisdom and Life, Making it Work for You*

(36) *Tom Feltenstein's Encyclopedia of Promotional Tactics*

(37) *Underdog Marketing: Strategies for Taking on the Big Guns*

Bill Main
(38) *Profit Tools™ – Front of the House Series*

(39) *Profit Tools™ – Back of the House Series*

(40) *Profit Tools™ – Top of the House Series*

Bill Marvin
(41) *Restaurant Basics: Why Guests Don't Come Back and What You Can Do About It,* 1992, John Wiley & Sons, Inc.

(42) *The Foolproof Foodservice Selection System: The Complete Manual for Creating a Quality Staff,* 1993, John Wiley & Sons

(43) *From Turnover to Teamwork: How to Build and Retain a Customer-Oriented Foodservice Staff,* 1994, John Wiley & Sons

(44) *50 Tips to Improve Your Tips: The Service Pro's Guide to Delighting Diners,* 1995, Prototype Restaurants

(45) *GBM/Guest-Based Marketing: How to Gain Foodservice Sales Without Losing Your Shirt,* 1997, John Wiley & Sons

(46) *Cashing in on Complaints: Turning Disappointed Diners into Gold,* 1997, Hospitality Masters Press

Ron Yudd
(47) *Successful Buffet Management,* 1990, Van Nostrand Reinhold

OFFERS YOU CAN'T REFUSE!

Our contributing authors are pleased to provide you with even more value by offering something for nothing! To request any of the information described below, just circle the corresponding number on the reader reply card or write directly to the author. (Note: SASE="self-addressed, stamped envelope.")

From Gloria Boileau

Would you like to achieve more prosperity with less work, ask for a free copy of **Ten Hot Tips for Applying Environmental Enhancement.** Circle **51** on the reply card or send a SASE to Boileau & Associates.

Create more impact – and more sales – through the appropriate use of color. For a free copy of Gloria's article, **How Color Sells,** circle **52** or send a SASE to Boileau & Associates.

Don't be inadvertently working against yourself. For a free copy of the article **Your Visual Impact Can Make or Break Your Career,** circle **53** or send a SASE to Boileau & Associates, PO Box 502, Cardiff-by-the-Sea, CA 92007.

From Susan Clarke

You don't have to be bad to get better, but to see just how good you really are, request a free copy of Susan's article, **21 Ways to Evaluate Team Performance.** Circle **54** or send a SASE to Motivation Unlimited!

Effective leaders have to create a team that wants to create change. To assist in this effort, request a free copy of Susan's article, **The Four Keys to Effective Change.** Circle **55** or send a SASE to Motivation Unlimited!, 2110 Sunset Cliffs Blvd., San Diego, CA 92107.

From Barry Cohen

To help you create a "WOW" environment that will energize you, your staff and your guests, get a free copy of Barry's checklist, **Ten Points to "WOW" Yourself.** Circle **56** or send a SASE to Barry Cohen, Old San Francisco Steak House, 9809 McCullough, San Antonio, TX 78216.

From Howard Cutson

Evaluate your bar operation the way your customers do with a free copy of Howard's **Five Senses Checklist™**. Circle **57** or send a SASE to Cutson Associates, 589 Atterbury Blvd., Hudson, OH 44236 and start improving your bar and lounge operations today!

From Tom Feltenstein

Tom Feltenstein's *Neighborhood Marketing Compass* will guide you easily through the seven steps of disciplined neighborhood marketing planning. Circle **58** or write Tom for your free copy.

For a free issue of Tom's potent newsletter, *Power Marketing Quarterly for the Foodservice Industry*, circle **59** or send a SASE to Feltenstein Partners, 44 Cocoanut Row, #T-5, Palm Beach, FL 36830.

From Peter Good

Take a positive step toward happier patrons with a free copy of *Five Steps to Memorable Guest Service*. Circle **60** or send a SASE to Peter Good Seminars, 14 W. Burlington, #200, LaGrange, IL 60525.

From Jim Laube

How well are you managing the financial side of your restaurant? Compare yourself with techniques used by the industry's most successful restaurateurs. For a free copy of *The Restaurant Operators Financial IQ Checklist,* circle **61** or send a SASE.

Are common foodservice misconceptions costing you money? To find out, get a free copy of *The Top 10 Myths of Foodservice Profitability.* Circle **62** or send a SASE to Center For Foodservice Education, 9801 Westheimer, Suite 302, Houston, TX 77042.

From Bill Main

Get a jump start on creating your own pre-shift sales briefing with a sample of Bill's *Pre-Shift Sales Briefing Form.* Circle **69** or send a SASE to Bill Main & Associates, 2220 St. George Lane, Suite 1, Chico, CA 95926.

From Phyllis Ann Marshall

Would you like to gain an edge over your competitors and make your restaurant more marketable? Circle **63** or send a SASE for a free copy of *Becoming a Brand - The Secret to an Unfair Advantage* to FoodPower, 2463 Irvine Ave., Ste E-1, Costa Mesa, CA 92627.

From Bill Marvin, The Restaurant Doctor™

If you have ever thought there **had** to be an easier way to communicate with your crew, circle **64** or send a SASE for a free copy of Bill's article, *Toward More Effective Staff Meetings.*

Are you intrigued by the idea of increasing productivity through *results-based position descriptions*? Circle **65** or send a SASE to Bill for a free example.

Keep your finger on the pulse of your service quality. Circle **70** or send a SASE to Bill for a free copy of his audio tape *Keeping Score on Service.*

Bill publishes his *Home Remedies newsletter*, full of practical insights for managers. Subscription is $24 a year but he will send you a year for free if you ask! Circle **66** or send a request to Effortless, Inc., PO Box 280, Gig Harbor, WA 98335.

From Rudy Miick

For a free *comprehensive operational assessment form,* circle **67** or send a SASE to Miick & Associates, 880 Sixth Street, Boulder, CO 80302. Better yet, return the completed assessment and Rudy will provide recommendations to enhance your performance!

From Ron Yudd

Jump-start your guest satisfaction with a copy of the handout from Ron's acclaimed seminar, *A Passion for Service.* Circle **68** or send a SASE to Ron Yudd at 10181 Nightingale Street, Gaithersburg, MD 20882.

Tested ideas from the leading speakers and consultants in the hospitality industry

Other books in the Hospitality Masters Series:

50 Proven Ways to Enhance Guest Service
50 Proven Ways to Build More Profitable Menus

Did you borrow this book? Do you want a copy of your own? Do you want extra copies for your staff and management? Do you want to take advantage of the incredible free offers from the contributing authors?

FREE OFFERS AND INFORMATION

Use this form to find out more about the contributing authors to this book or to request the free material offered in Appendix C. Allow 30 days for delivery.

01	02	03	04	05	06	07	08	09	10
11	12	13	14	15	16	17	18	19	20
21	22	23	24	25	26	27	28	29	30
31	32	33	34	35	36	37	38	39	40
41	42	43	44	45	46	47	48	49	50
51	52	53	54	55	56	57	58	59	60
61	62	63	64	65	66	67	68	69	70
71	72	73	74	75	76	77	78	79	80
81	82	83	84	85	86	87	88	89	90

SEND BOOKS AND INFORMATION TO:

Name _____

Company _____

Address _____

City _____ State _____ Zip _____

Phone _____ Fax _____

e-mail _____

BOOK ORDER

YES! I want to invest in my future success and have personal copies of the following books in the Hospitality Masters Series:

_____ *50 Proven Ways to Build Restaurant Sales & Profit*

_____ *50 Proven Ways to Build More Profitable Menus*

_____ *50 Proven Ways to Enhance Guest Service*

1-14 copies: $14.95 each plus postage & handling*

15+ copies: call for discount information

POSTAGE & HANDLING MUST BE ADDED TO ALL ORDERS
Figure postage & handling at the greater of $5.00* or 6% of the total book order.

Total No. Copies _____

Total Amount of Order: $ _____

Method of Payment: ☐ Check ☐ Money Order ☐ Visa ☐ MC ☐ Amex ☐ Discover/Novus

Account No. _____

Expires _____ Signature _____

*Canadian funds: $19.95 + postage & handling (greater of $6.00 or 8% of book order)
Allow 30 days for delivery on all orders

return to:

HOSPITALITY MASTERS PRESS
PO Box 280 • Gig Harbor, WA 98335

For faster service, FAX your request toll-free to (888) 767-1055